ALSIP-MERRIONETTE PARK LIBRARY
DISCARDED

W9-BTL-970

STAMP
COLLECTING

DATE DUE

JUL 1 4 2004

GAYLORD   PRINTED IN U.S.A

GE   ION

LOVELAND, COLORADO

Copyright © 1999 by Stephen R. Datz

All rights reserved under the Universal and Pan American Conventions. This work, or any portion thereof, may not be reproduced or transmitted in any form, by any means, electronic or mechanical, including photocopying and recording, or by any information storage or retrieval system, without the express written permission of the author in each specific instance.

First Printing: June 1999
Second Printing: March 2000
Third Printing: July 2001

ISBN: 0-88219-030-X

Cover design: Mike Jenson

Manufactured in the United States of America

Published by General Philatelic Corporation
Division of General Trade Corporation
Post Office Box 402
Loveland, Colorado 80539

Philatelic Books by Stephen R. Datz

THE BUYER'S GUIDE

CATALOGUE OF ERRORS ON U.S. STAMPS

THE DATZ PHILATELIC INDEX

ON THE ROAD

STAMP COLLECTING

STAMP INVESTING

TOP DOLLAR PAID

THE WILD SIDE

CONTENTS

CONTENTS

Acknowledgments

Thanks are due James Magruder, Bill Welch, and Wayne Youngblood for generously taking the time to answer questions, provide suggestions, and clarify details.

Thanks also to Ken Beiner for his assistance with the illustrations and for his ongoing insights and suggestions as the project progressed. I'm grateful to Judy Waller for proofreading and to Mike Jenson for his assistance with the graphics.

I am especially grateful to Dorothy Harris for her guidance, encouragement, and support, without which this book would not have been reality.

Once again, thanks to my wife Susan, who helped keep the project on track and pointed in the right direction.

FOREWORD

We put a stamp on a letter, mail it, and two or three days later it arrives. We do it all the time and never give it a second thought. It's all so simple. But it was not always that way.

There was a time when a person had to present each letter at the post office so that its postage could be calculated; a separate fee existed for each destination. And the cost could be as high as half a day's wages.

Sir Rowland Hill

Sir Rowland Hill is credited with inventing the postage stamp in the late 1830s as part of his plan to reform the British postal system and establish uniform postage rates. At the time, the cost of sending a letter was calculated by a combination weight and distance, resulting in a hodgepodge of fees, one from every individual point in Great Britain to every other point. The expense of sending a letter was so great that the average person rarely sent one.

People depended on writing to communicate in those days. There was no telephone, fax, or e-mail. And the high cost of postage inhibited communication, both business and personal. At the time, people had the option of prepaying letters—in which case the postmaster marked the letter paid by pen or handstamp—or sending them collect, which many did. Senders felt that since recipients were the ones who benefitted from receiving a letter, they should pay for it. If a recipient refused a letter—which often happened—the post office was out the cost of transporting it.

Rowland Hill proposed a uniform fee—one penny—for any letter sent anywhere in the kingdom, and that the fee be collected in advance. He reasoned that a uniform rate structure would reduce paperwork, increase efficiency, and encourage people to send more letters. Hill proposed that a small piece of paper evidencing pre-payment of postage be attached to each letter at the time of mailing, and thus the postage stamp was born. Stamps also would tighten accountability, since postmasters would have to account for every stamp sold. Under the previous system of marking letters "paid" by penstroke, there was little to prevent a postmaster from pocketing postage. Prepayment of postage also would eliminate the inefficient collect system. What really made Hill's proposal revolutionary was his recommendation to slash the cost of mailing a letter from an average cost of nine pence to one penny—an eighty-nine percent reduction! Critics ridiculed Hill and warned that if implemented, his ridiculous scheme would lead to the ruination of the postal system. But Great Britain really had no other choice. The existing postal system was so burdensome on the public, so constraining on commerce, that it had begun to be a drag on the economy. So they gave Hill's plan a try, and to their amazement, it worked. The volume of mail increased steadily and the postal system did not collapse as predicted. Queen Victoria knighted Hill for his contribution to creating the modern postal system. But philatelists around the world remember Sir Rowland Hill for another reason—inventing the postage stamp.

The world's first postage stamp (1840) featured a finely engraved profile of the young Queen Victoria together with the words "Postage" and "One Penny." Printed in black, it became known as the Penny Black. The name "Great Britain" did not appear on the Penny Black, only the simple, elegant portrait of Queen Victoria. To this day, Great Britain remains the only nation in the world that does not print its name on its postage stamps. Nor is it required to, a tribute to the contribution it made by introducing the modern postage stamp.

The Penny Black at left; contemporary British stamp at right.

Before 1845, the United States shared Great Britain's confusing system of hodgepodge postal rates based loosely on distance and weight. In 1845, Congress followed Britain's lead and established uniform rates of postage for the United States. Letters traveling less than 300 miles cost 5 cents per half ounce; those traveling farther than 300 miles cost 10 cents per half ounce. In 1847, the United States issued its first postage stamps, although prior to that time several postmasters had issued provisionals (stamps issued locally by postmasters) as the success of the Penny Black became known.

Sir Rowland Hill's idea caught on quickly, and in no time nations all over the world began issuing postage stamps. And not long after, people began collecting them. They collected stamps because of their artwork and beauty and because stamps piqued their curiosity about far off and mysterious-sounding places—Mauritius, St. Helena, Sierra Leone—places they had never heard of, places they never suspected existed, places they suddenly hungered to know more about. Stamps provided tangible evidence of a broader world, something one could hold in their hand from far-off and exotic places such as Mozambique, Manchukuo, and Tristan Da Cunha. These elements of beauty and mystery fascinated early collectors, and continue to fascinate collectors to this day.

Stamp collectors know an amazing amount of trivia about world geography and history, all from postage stamps. They know these facts because stamps, especially commemoratives, reveal the essential kernels of a nation's history, geography, and notable personalities. They are windows into its culture. Every time one

First postage stamps of the United States.

turns the pages of a stamp album, history unfolds. Kings, presidents, and dictators. Heros, despots, and idealogues. Scientists, explorers, and great thinkers. Authors, musicians, and artists. Events, places, flora and fauna. They're all waiting to be discovered and enjoyed on postage stamps.

PHILATELY

The term philately (stamp collecting) comes from the Greek *philos* (loving) and *ateleia* (exempt from tax), and refers to the fact that a postage stamp prepays a fee, rendering a letter free of tax (so to speak) to the recipient. Philately is more encompassing than just collecting and mounting stamps. It includes an interest in and the study of all things stamp related—covers, postal history, stamp design and production, and so forth. It's a widespread and well-established hobby, with collectors in every nation of the world and roots going back more than 150 years. A highly organized and stable international market gives stamps liquidity matched by few other hobbies.

The United States Postal Service estimates that 22 million Americans collect stamps. Most of these are casual collectors who don't necessarily save every stamp issued, belong to a philatelic society, or attend stamp shows. You may be one of these and not realize it. Of the 22 million, perhaps 250,000 are serious collectors who own albums, belong to one or more national philatelic societies, or subscribe to one or more philatelic newspapers or magazines.

This book is organized to introduce you to the hobby of stamp collecting and provide insight into how stamp collectors think. As you proceed through the chapters you will acquire the essential vocabulary, learn about the essential tools, learn how to use a stamp catalogue, learn how to get started, learn how to protect your stamps, and learn how to access additional philatelic resources. By the time you're through you will have a grasp of the fundamentals. The text is followed by a Resource Guide and a Bibliography. The Resource Guide lists sources for stamps, supplies, periodicals, museums, philatelic libraries, and stamp organizations. The Bibliography contains titles of books that delve more deeply into specific subjects.

Stamps are small in relation to most other objects, and because stamps are small, stamp collectors tend to be detail oriented. They pay attention to every element of a stamp—type of printing, type of paper, type of watermark, type of perforations, centering, and hinging—all of which are important and have a bearing on value.

Stamp collectors tend to be precise and analytical. Philately has evolved an extensive technical vocabulary to describe detail. The basic terms are defined in the next chapter, "Essential Vocabulary." Additional terms are used throughout the text. Consult the Glossary at the end of the book as you encounter them.

Stamp collectors possess inquiring minds. Curiosity and acquisitiveness drive them. When a collector looks at a stamp, he or she wants to know, what is it, where it comes from, when it was made, which details—if any—distinguish it from others of similar appearance, if it is rare, if it is in premium condition, if it has been altered, and how much it is worth. He wants to know about its place in history and its place in his collection. He wants to know as much as he can about a stamp.

Most of us use stamps daily, or at least receive mail bearing stamps, but never give them much thought. By the time you have finished this book, you will understand how collectors perceive these small bits of paper, and you, too, will see stamps differently. Perhaps you will be bitten by the collecting bug. Perhaps, the next time you hold a stamp in your hands, you, too, will regard it as a small treasure.

ESSENTIAL VOCABULARY

Below appear the terms that you will encounter most frequently and with which you should become conversant in order to carry on a conversation with other collectors and with stamp dealers.

TYPES OF STAMPS

A stamp is a bit of paper that evidences the prepayment of a fee, most often postage. Basic types of stamps include:

Postage stamp—the most common type of stamp, used to evidence prepayment of postage. The term "postage stamp" distinguishes it from other types of stamps such as revenue stamps or savings stamps.

Definitive—issued for use on everyday mail. Usually issued in a series of various denominations and available over an extended period of time. Definitives are also known as regular issues.

Commemorative—a special stamp issued to honor an event, personality, anniversary, or topic, and typically available for only a limited time, usually six to eighteen months.

Special stamp—or special occasion stamp. Not really a definitive or commemorative, examples include Love stamps, and holiday stamps such as Christmas, Hanukkah, and Kwanzaa stamps.

Airmail—a stamp intended primarily for use on airmail.

Parcel post stamp—a stamp intended for use on parcel post.

Special delivery—a stamp for use on special delivery mail.

Official—a stamp valid for use only by a government agency and intended for use only on official mail.

Postage due—a stamp used to show that postage was underpaid by the sender and postage is due from the addressee.

Semi-postal—a stamp for which only part of the purchase price applies toward postage; the balance is collected for some other purpose, often a charitable cause. Semi-postals are usually denominated by two figures; the first is the amount valid for postage, the second is the amount allocated for the other purpose, e.g., 50c+20c. In some cases, such as the U.S. Breast Cancer Research stamp of 1998, the denominations are not printed.

Non-denominated—a stamp without a numerical denomination. The denomination is often represented by a letter such as A, B, or C, or by other inscription. Non-denominated stamps are most often transitional issues printed when a rate increase is anticipated but before the actual new rate is known.

Computer vended postage—stamps dispensed by vending machines that imprint the denomination at the time the stamp is vended, usually on security paper containing a pre-printed background.

Postal stationery—stationery sold by the post office usually, but not always, with postage imprinted. Postal stationery includes postal cards, stamped envelopes, and aerogrammes (air letters).

Cut square—the upper right portion of a piece of postal stationery containing the printed stamp and paper immediately surrounding it, often with room to show the postmark, if present.

Meter stamp—evidence that postage has been paid, applied by postage meter device such as manufactured by the Pitney-Bowes Company.

Revenue—a stamp used to show the payment of a tax or fee. Sometimes referred to as a fiscal. Examples include waterfowl hunting stamps, documentary stamps, playing card stamps, and cigarette stamps. Postage stamps are sometimes used to evidence payment of revenue fees, as often seen in countries of the British Commonwealth.

Cinderella—a general, all-encompassing term applied to any stamp-like item not valid for postage such as exhibition labels, Christmas seals, parodies, imitations, and advertising fantasy issues.

Sheet stamp at left; pair of coil stamps at right.

Sheet stamp—a stamp issued in sheet form. Sheet stamps usually have perforations on all four sides, unless the stamp was issued imperforate or unless the stamp borders the edge of a pane and contains a straight edge.

Coil stamp—a stamp issued in roll form. Coil stamps have straight edges on opposite parallel sides.

Booklet stamp—a stamp issued in booklet form. Booklet stamps often, but not always have one or more straight-edged sides. Often bound between cardstock covers by staples, thread, or glue, but lately sold in panes of self-adhesive stamps that can be folded for carrying in purse or wallet. Individual sheetlets of booklet stamps are known as booklet panes.

Self-adhesive—a stamp that can be peeled from its backing and attached to a cover (envelope) without being moistened. Stamps with traditional gum that requires moistening are known as water-activated stamps.

Test stamp—a dummy stamp used to test or set up stamp vending machines.

Souvenir sheet—a sheet, usually small, containing one or more stamps, usually bearing a commemorative marginal inscription, and usually issued in connection with some special event or occasion. Stamps in souvenir sheets are valid for postage.

PRINTING METHODS

Intaglio—also known as engraved printing. A method of printing in which the design is engraved (recessed) into a metal plate. Ink fills the recesses and when the stamp is printed, forms small ridges on the paper. Intaglio printing can be identified by magnifying glass or by running a finger over the surface of the stamp and feeling the ridges. U.S. currency is printed by the intaglio method.

Lithography—sometimes referred to as offset printing. A printing process using photographically etched plates. In some cases the image from the metal plate is offset onto a rubber-like blanket before being impressed onto the paper, hence the term offset printing. In lithography, images are broken up into a series of dots to achieve tonal gradation. Color lithography involves mingling areas of dots from several plates, each printing a separate color, in order to achieve the effect of full color. The dot structure is visible under a magnifying glass.

Photogravure—also known as gravure printing. Like lithography, a gravure plate is made by the photosensitive process; in photogravure, however, the ink lies in small recesses and is very thinly applied. Tones are achieved by varying the depth of the recesses and thickness of the ink. The image is broken up into a series of fine points that keep the paper from being pressed into the recesses. The dot structure in photogravure is usually much finer than that of lithography. The difference is apparent under a 10-power magnifying glass.

Typographed—also known as letterpress printing. The oldest form of printing. A method of printing in which the ink sits atop raised type and is transferred directly to paper.

BASIC TERMS

Mint—a stamp that has not been used (cancelled). Often used in a stricter sense to mean a never-hinged, post-office-fresh stamp; however, there is no hard and fast rule.

Unused—a stamp that has not been used (cancelled). Although the term can be applied to any uncancelled stamp, either with or without gum, it is frequently used—mostly in auction catalogs and advertising—to mean an uncancelled stamp lacking original gum, and in that sense has become nearly idiomatic. When using an auction catalogue or buying from an advertisement, be sure you understand the connotation of the term as it relates to the offering, because a stamp without original gum is worth considerably less than one with original gum. More about this in the chapter "Condition and Grading."

Used—a stamp that has been cancelled.

Postally used—a stamp that has been used on mail as originally intended, as opposed to being cancelled to order (CTO) or used for revenue purposes. Advanced collectors generally prefer postally used stamps to CTOs or those bearing revenue cancels. They feel postally used stamps are more legitimate, having performed the duty for which they were intended. Postally used stamps are generally worth more than CTOs or revenue-cancelled examples of the same stamp.

Cancelled to order (CTO)—a term used to describe the mass cancellation (typically applied to full sheets by printing press) of remainders of mint stamps, which are then usually sold at a discount from face value. The United States Postal Service (USPS) does not sell CTOs; some—but not all—foreign postal administrations do. CTOs most often appear in inexpensive mixtures, packets, and approvals. CTOs are generally easy to spot. A neatly applied, nonobliterative, printed cancel on a foreign stamp with full original gum is a dead giveaway. Note the exact, identical wording and placement of cancellations in the illustration.

City and state
precancel.

Bars-only
precancel.

Service-inscribed
precancel.

Precancel—a stamp cancelled before being sold and most often used by bulk mailers. Precancels save the postal service the trouble and cost of having to postmark a multitude of individual pieces of bulk mail. Traditionally, precancels contained the name of the mailer's city and state between two parallel bars. In the 1970s the style evolved into just a pair of black bars. Later, even the bars were omitted and most precancels today contain no apparent cancellation. Instead, they are "service-inscribed" according to their intended use, e.g., "bulk rate" or "presorted standard." Service-inscribed stamps are commonly used on junk mail because marketing surveys have shown that recipients open a higher percentage of mail when it bears a stamp (as opposed to a printed indicia or postage meter). Collectors of traditional (city and state inscribed) precancels generally don't expect gum on their stamps. However, collectors of mint service-inscribed precancels prefer that they possess full original gum.

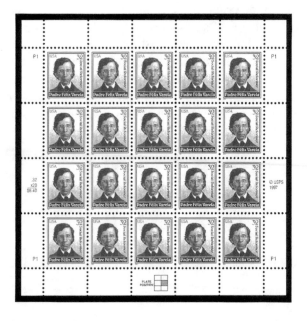

Compact sheet—a pane of modern U.S. postage stamps containing fewer than the traditional 50 or 100 stamps—often only fifteen or twenty stamps—and in some cases with a marginal inscription, decoration, or illustration. Most modern U.S. sheet stamps are issued in compact sheet format. The diagram in the bottom selvage shows the position of the pane on the press sheet.

Pane—the technical term for a finished "sheet" of stamps as purchased across a post office counter, as distinct from a press sheet, which usually contains multiple panes of stamps.

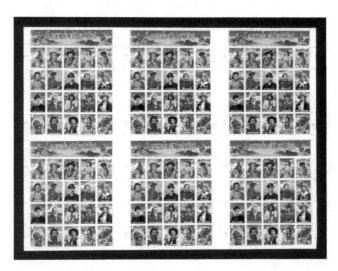

Press sheet—also often referred to as an uncut press sheet. A press sheet contains multiple panes of stamps in the form in which they came off the printing press.

Perforations—also known as perfs. The rows of holes between stamps that facilitate their separation. Holes not completely punched through a stamp's paper are known as blind perfs.

Imperforate—a stamp lacking perforations. Before the invention of perforating equipment, stamps were issued imperforate and separated by cutting. Edges on stamps lacking perforations, such as coil stamps and booklet stamps, are referred to as "straight edges" rather than being imperforate.   Perforated stamps un-intentionally issued without perforations are known as errors.

Rouletted stamp at left; serpentine die-cut stamp at right.

Roulette—a philatelic term referring to a series of slits applied between stamps to facilitate separation.

Die cut—most self-adhesive stamps are die cut during manufacture to permit separation.   Some die cuts are simple straight lines; others are serpentine or saw-toothed in appearance to simulate perforations.

Cover—a philatelic term for envelope, usually with a stamp or stamps attached.   The term "cover" implies that the envelope has gone through the mail.   A stamp attached to a cover is referred to as being on cover.

First day cover (FDC)—a cover bearing a stamp that has been postmarked on the first day it was available for sale to the public.

Selvage—the marginal area surrounding a sheet or pane of stamps. Sometimes spelled selvedge.

Cachet—pronounced ka-shay; a decorative illustration usually appearing on the left side of a cover, usually in connection with a first day of issue or special event. Cachets may be printed, rubber stamped, hand painted, or applied by other means.

Block—four or more stamps arranged in a rectangle.

Plate block—a block of stamps on whose selvage appears the printing plate number or numbers.

Plate number coil (PNC)—a coil stamp on which a small printing plate number appears at the bottom. Plate numbers appear at the bottom of stamps at predetermined intervals, e.g., every 24th or 52nd stamp. PNCs are usually collected in strips of three or five with the numbered stamp occupying the center position in the strip.

Line pair—a pair of coil stamps on which a line appears between stamps. On engraved, rotary-press coil stamps, the lines are created by ink that fills the space where the curved plates join, which is then printed in the same fashion as ink from recesses in an intaglio stamp design.

Se-tenant—two or more stamp of different design printed next to one another on a pane of stamps, a souvenir sheet, a booklet, or a coil.

Tête-bêche—pronounced tet-besh, two adjacent stamps, one of which is inverted in relation to the other.

Tagged—a stamp possessing a luminescent coating applied during printing. Usually invisible to the naked eye, tagging can be observed under ultraviolet light. Tagging may cover all or part of a stamp.

Overprint—printing applied to a stamp after regular production for any number of reasons: to denote a special purpose (such as airmail), to commemorate something, or as a control measure. An overprint intended to change the face value of a stamp is known as a surcharge. Overprints are not cancellations.

ESSENTIAL TOOLS

Stamp Tongs. A pair of stamp tongs is the most basic philatelic tool. Stamp tongs provide more dexterity than human fingers, and they eliminate the possibility of damage from rough handling, moisture, oil, and the like. They come in a variety of styles and range in price from a couple of dollars on up. All dealers stock them. Don't use manicure tweezers or any other tool not specifically intended for handling stamps; some have sharp edges or ridges for gripping, which can cause damage when used to pick up stamps. As condition is the key element of stamp value, it is essential to guard against careless handling that might cause damage, however slight.

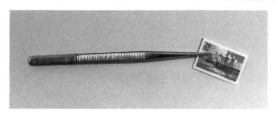

Stamp tongs.

Perforation Gauge. It is nearly impossible to accurately measure perforations without a perforation gauge.

When any of several elements (perforations, watermark, color, paper, type of printing press) differ on stamps of the same design, each is considered a distinct, collectible variety. A perforation gauge is used to measure a stamp's perforations and thus distinguish one perforation variety from another. Most stamps exist

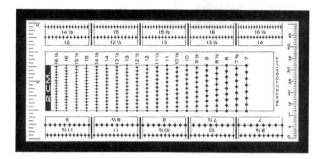

Perforation gauge (reduced from actual size).

perforated in only a single way, so measurement isn't necessary. A perforation gauge makes it easy to identify those that exist in several perforation varieties.

Perforations are measured by the number of holes that appear within a space of 2 centimeters. Perforated 10 means that 10 perforation holes appear in 2 centimeters; perforated 10½ means 10½ holes per 2 centimeters, and so forth. When perforations are of the same size on all sides of a stamp, the measurement is expressed as "perforated 11," or whatever gauge number is appropriate. Perforations on parallel sides of a stamp are the same (except in a few rare cases), but sometimes differ horizontally and vertically, which case they are known as compound perforations, and the measurement is expressed in the form "perforated 10½x11," with the first numeral referring to the horizontal gauge and the second to the vertical. Collectors generally shorten the word "perforated" and say "perf 11," or "perf 10½x11," and so forth.

Ninety-nine percent of perforation measurements are expressed to the nearest half or quarter hole, i.e., 10½ or 10¼. Some catalogue publishers have begun expressing perforation measurements for newly issued stamps decimally, e.g., perforated 11.2. Wisely, they've chosen not to revise previously published measurements into decimal expression, which would result in endless confusion. However, since the trend for new issues seems to be decimal expression, it makes sense to obtain a gauge that measures in both fractions and decimals. *Linn's Stamp News* Multi-gauge is one of the best and costs only a few dollars.

This example is perforated 11x12. Note the different spacing of perforations horizontally and vertically.

The John Paul Jones commemorative, issued in 1979, exists perforated 11; perforated 11x12; and perforated 12. The first two types are worth less than half a dollar each; the perforated 12 variety is worth about $2,000 mint and $1,000 used, so it pays to be aware of differences in perforation.

Watermark tray and fluid.

Watermark Detector. A stamp's watermark—or lack of watermark—is just as important as its perforations. A watermark is a mark impressed in paper during its manufacture while pulp is wet and being rolled out. The impressed mark is thinner than surrounding paper and, therefore, appears lighter. Watermarked paper is employed in stamp production as a security measure. You may have noticed watermarks on certain types stationery; it becomes visible when held up to light. A variety of images have

A watermark becomes visible when immersed in fluid.

been used as watermarks on stamps, including letters, crests, and geometric patterns. Some stamp watermarks are visible when held up to light and viewed from the back, but most are not because of the small size of stamps and the opacity of printing ink. Watermarks on U.S. stamps are almost impossible to see without a watermark detector.

The traditional watermark detector is a black tray in which a stamp is placed face down and covered with watermark fluid causing the watermark to become visible. Tray and fluid cost only a few dollars.

CAUTION: Do not use water in a watermark detector. You'll lose the gum on mint stamps and greatly diminish their value. Use only watermark fluid designed specifically for use with stamps. Watermark fluid is inexpensive and available at any stamp dealer or by mail order from any stamp supply company.

TIP: A little fluid goes a long way. Put the stamp in the tray first, then add only as much fluid as necessary to moisten it and reveal the watermark. It is not necessary to drown the stamp in a tray full of fluid, then have to struggle to pour the excess back into the bottle without spilling it.

Watermark fluid doesn't dissolve stamp gum and it dries almost instantly. Some individuals use lighter fluid in watermark trays. It works just fine; however, it leaves a slight, almost imperceptible oily residue, so it's best to avoid it. The inks of some British Commonwealth stamps are soluble in watermark fluid, so it's wise to consult a stamp catalogue before immersing these kinds of stamps. Watermark trays are also used to detect damage (thins, creases, etc.) and repairs, but more about that later. Checking for watermarks may sound a bit complicated, but in practice it isn't.

Double line (left), single line (right).

The United States used watermarked paper (with letters as illustrated above) for postage stamps between the years 1895 and 1915, so there's no need to check earlier or later stamps. Many foreign nations still use watermarked paper. Specialists prize inverted watermarks, omitted watermarks, and erroneously watermarked stamps (such as the 1938 U.S. $1 Woodrow Wilson postage stamp inadvertently printed on paper watermarked USIR (United States Internal Revenue) intended for revenue stamps. The error stamp currently is worth about $300 mint and $70 used.

Optical-electric watermark detectors eliminate the need for fluid. Some collectors prefer them for that reason; however, optical-electric watermark detectors are costly ($100 and up) and work best on mint never-hinged stamps and stamps without gum. Hinge remnants and disturbed gum tend to obscure watermarks and faults. Most collectors prefer the traditional method because it is inexpensive, portable, and invariably gives a reliable result.

Magnifying Glass. A good magnifying glass or jeweler's loupe is indispensable. It should be at least 10 power to adequately view secret marks, type markings, and other small details.

Album. Stamp collections are generally housed in albums, which range from entry-level basic to the highly specialized and expensive. Albums protect stamps, serve as means of organizing them, and are a convenient way to view and enjoy them. Most albums feature printed illustrations on each page to indicate the

placement of stamps. Top-of-the-line hingeless albums come with plastic mounts preinstalled, so that all one need do is insert stamps in their appropriate spaces. Albums exist for nearly all countries, and for U.S. stamps and U.S. specialties such as plate blocks and plate number coils. The best albums are loose-leaf to accommodate supplement pages, which album companies publish (usually annually) to enable collectors to keep their collections up to date. Some album pages are printed on acid-free or archival paper. More about albums in "Getting Started."

Don't be hasty or impulsive when choosing an album, especially an expensive one. Talk to other collectors and get the benefit of their experience before buying.

CAUTION: Never house stamps in variety-store photo albums, especially those with self-adhesive or wax-backed pages. The wax penetrates the stamps and in time ruins them, especially in hot climates. Even photo-albums with "low-tack" adhesive can damage stamps over time. A good rule of thumb is, if something wasn't meant for stamps, don't use it.

TIP: Experienced collectors prefer album pages printed on one side rather than two sides because facing pages loaded with stamps tend to catch on one another as pages are turned. If you must use double-sided pages, insert glassine interleaves between them to avoid damage. They're available from stamp dealers and album publishers.

Advanced collectors, specialists, and exhibitors often prefer to make their own album pages with as many or as few stamps per page as seems appropriate, and with as much or as little text as serves their purpose. Most album manufacturers offer quadrille-lined blank pages (a background of faintly printed square or rectangular lines), which make designing a layout easy. A variety of computer software for making album pages is also on the market. Check advertising in philatelic periodicals for the latest types.

Albums for housing covers usually contain loose-leaf pages with clear plastic pockets into which covers can be inserted for display. The best are made of mylar. Those made of vinyl treated with softening agents (visible as an oily iridescent film; the more softener, the more iridescence), should be avoided as these agents have been known to leach the color out of some printing inks and to discolor stamps.

Stamp mount (left); stamp hinges (right).

Mounts. Until the late twentieth century, stamp hinges were the mount of choice. Modern hinges consist of a bit of glassine lightly gummed on one side. The hinge is folded, usually about one-third of the way from the top, the smaller flap lightly moistened (too much moisture will make the hinge difficult to remove later), and attached to the stamp near its top edge. The larger flap is moistened and attached to the album page. Hinges work well and are still the mount of choice for low-cost stamps and used stamps. Few collectors use them for mint never-hinged stamps because they leave a mark on gum when removed. Until the mid-twentieth century, no one paid much attention to hinge marks, but once the hobby began insisting on pristine gum, hinges for mint stamps, especially expensive ones, fell out of favor.

Today, the mount of choice for mint stamps is the plastic mount. Plastic mounts are easy to use, protect stamps from hinging, frame them nicely against an album page, and lend a polished look to their presentation. Plastic mounts come in a variety of sizes to meet any conceivable need. Several different styles and brands exist. They're available from most dealers.

Odds and Ends. Glassine envelopes are used for storing stamps. They're inexpensive and come in variety of sizes. Never use wax paper or plastic kitchen wrap to house or store stamps. They usually end up doing more harm than good.

Stock books are handy for organizing stamps awaiting mounting and for storing duplicates. Stock book pages consist of horizontal pockets created from manila, glassine, or clear plastic into which stamps can be slipped. Stock books are available in a variety of sizes.

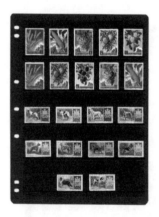

Display-style stock sheet (left); manila stock sheet (right).

Stock sheets are the loose-leaf version of stock book pages. They come punched for three-ring binders and several other types of binders. Display-style stock sheets are made of black or white card or plastic stock on which as few as one or as many as fourteen clear plastic pockets have been attached. Some collectors use display-style stock sheets to house their collections instead of traditional album pages. They like the flexibility and convenience of stock sheets, and, indeed, there is much to recommend this system. Manila stock sheets are less expensive than display-style stock sheets and are often used to store duplicates.

Stock cards are small versions of stock sheets, and are available in a variety of sizes, the most common of which measures 3¼x5½ inches and contains either one or two rows of pockets. They're useful for housing high-quality duplicates.

Plastic sleeves, sealed on three sides and open on the fourth, are used to house covers. They come in a variety of sizes. The best are made of mylar or polyethylene, both of which are much more inert than softened vinyl. Mylar sleeves are clear and rigid. Poly sleeves are slightly grayish in appearance, floppy rather than rigid, and weigh less if shipping or traveling is a consideration.

A color identification chart is useful, especially for those just getting started. Stanley Gibbons manufactures one of the best.

Pages from two identification guides.

An identification guide is worth its weight in gold because before you can look a stamp up in a catalogue, you need to know its country of origin. Identifying stamps inscribed in Arabic, Chinese, Japanese, Korean, or cyrillic is especially frustrating. Just because a stamp is inscribed in cyrillic doesn't mean it comes from Russia. It might come from any of more than a dozen countries such as Armenia, Montenegro, or Bulgaria. You could spend all day flipping through a catalogue and still not know where your stamp came from. Identification guides group illustrations of difficult-to-identify stamps together by inscriptions, by heads (of state), by numerals, and by pictures. It takes only seconds to identify a stamp using one. Identification guides also contain a glossary of foreign expressions that appear on stamps such as *autopaketti* (inscription on Finnish parcel post stamps) and *tasa* (inscription on postage due stamps of Uruguay) to make identification of specific kinds of stamps easy. Several brands exist. Most dealers carry at least one.

Ultraviolet light is used to detect luminescent coatings on stamps. Since the late 1960s a variety of luminescent coatings have been utilized on stamps to trigger automated facing and cancelling equipment. The stamps we use every day contain some type of luminescence, either in the paper or printed atop the design. This invisible coating, referred to by collectors as tagging, is visible under ultraviolet light, and is important to the specialist. However, unless tagging varieties are important to you, an ultraviolet light may not be worth the expense.

TIP: If you buy an ultraviolet light, get a portable model that fluoresces *both* longwave and shortwave ultraviolet light. Savvy collectors favor the type used by gem and mineral collectors.

Philately has been blessed with a wealth of literature few other hobbies can match. During the past 150 years, thousands of knowledgeable collectors from all over the world have written books on just about every aspect of philately. No matter how esoteric or obscure your area of interest, you will almost certainly be able to find a philatelic reference specific to the subject—airmail stamps, postal cards, territorial post offices, Zeppelin mail, even books devoted to the study of a single stamp such as Carroll Chase's exhaustive study of the U.S. three-cent 1851-1857 issue. You name it, there's likely a book on it. Out-of-print books are available from philatelic literature dealers, or you can borrow them from philatelic libraries. Consult the Resource Guide for more information.

Ken Wood's three-volume work *This is Philately* is a wonderfully comprehensive encyclopedia of philately, and an excellent and recommended general reference. It is scarcely possible to think of a term or subject not covered in its thorough 878 pages. Beginner and old-hand alike find it useful.

The most basic reference work is the stamp catalogue. Every collector should own at least one. Catalogues are so important that the next chapter is devoted entirely to them.

Never hesitate to invest in books. An old maxim counsels, "Buy the book, then buy the stamp." A kernel of knowledge can mean the difference between buying or selling a stamp for pennies versus hundreds of dollars. Books are truly worth their weight in gold, not only in terms of knowledge, but as collectors' items themselves. Philatelic specialty books are usually printed in small press runs, typically 100 to 2,000 copies. They're often expensive new, but once out of print, sell for a multiple of their original cover price.

Subscribe to at least one philatelic newspaper. It's the best way to keep current on the hobby. *Linn's Stamp News* and *Mekeel's & Stamps Magazine* are published weekly; *Stamp Collector* is published bi-monthly. They feature news, calendars of forthcoming issues, schedules of stamp shows across the nation, and loads of advertisements with current market prices. *Global Stamp News*, a hefty newspaper published monthly, is a must for anyone who collects foreign stamps. *Scott Stamp Monthly* is also highly recommended. It's loaded with articles of interest to every collector from beginner to advanced. In addition, dozens of specialized societies publish monthly or quarterly journals. Foremost among them is the monthly magazine, the *American Philatelist*, published by the American Philatelic Society. Check the Resource Guide for specifics.

STAMP CATALOGUES

A stamp catalogue is the basic reference to which all collectors turn time and time again. The term "catalogue" in philatelic parlance takes on the connotation of a reference work rather than a publication from which one might order something, such as a Sears catalog or an L.L. Bean catalog. It is usually—but not always—spelled "catalogue" rather than "catalog," perhaps to reinforce its role as a reference. Stamp catalogues provide two primary types of information: technical and pricing.

Scott Publishing Company publishes a highly respected annual catalogue, the *Scott Standard Postage Catalogue,* that lists, illustrates, and prices virtually every general variety of postage stamp in the world. Scott also publishes the *Specialized Catalogue of U.S. Stamps and Covers*, which lists, illustrates, and prices every U.S. postage stamp as well as Christmas seals, revenue stamps, proofs, essays, and just about anything else stamp-related of significance or value. It is indispensable for the U.S. collector.

Krause Publications also publishes a U.S. stamp catalogue, the *Krause-Minkus Standard Catalogue of U.S. Stamps.* It lists, illustrates, and prices U.S. stamps as well, but in addition, provides historical background nuggets with each stamp, which many, including beginners, find especially informative and useful.

Several other firms publish U.S. stamp catalogues or combination catalogue/pricelists. The *Brookman, Harris*, and *Mystic* catalogues each use the Scott numbering system under license from Scott, and each has its own constituency. In addition

Typical catalogue pages.

to these, the Postal Service publishes a pocket guide, *The Postal Service Guide to U.S. Stamps,* which is noteworthy because it is illustrated in color. Catalogues are available from stamp dealers, bookstores, and at most libraries.

If you develop an interest in collecting a foreign country's stamps, consider buying a specialized catalogue for that country. As a rule, the most comprehensive foreign specialized catalogues are published in the countries of their stamps' origin. For example, *Gibbons* is the undisputed authority for Great Britain; *Michel* for Germany; *Yvert* or *Ceres* for France; *Bolaffi* for Italy; *Zumstein* for Switzerland, and *Edefil* for Spain. Foreign specialized catalogues cover the stamps of their nations in exquisite detail, listing, illustrating, and pricing stamps that are too esoteric for general worldwide catalogues. If you decide to specialize in a foreign country, it is wise to have one of these, even if it's a few years old, just for the illustrations and technical information, which never change. The only drawback to most foreign specialized catalogues is that they are published in the language of their country of origin, not in English. Still, since most listings are illustrated and described in philatelic shorthand, they are reasonably comprehensible. Check with your local dealer for these.

Specialty catalogues focus more narrowly still, providing highly detailed information that general catalogues do not. Examples include *Durland Standard Plate Number Catalog* (for plate blocks) and the *Scott First Day Cover Catalogue* (for FDCs). Many others exist.

The first function of a catalogue is identification. Before using any catalogue, read the introduction carefully. You'll save yourself a lot of time and trouble. Although listings are user-friendly, they contain information of a technical nature often not understood by those unfamiliar with the protocols and nuances of philately.

In worldwide stamp catalogues, stamps are organized by country, and listed chronologically. Within a country, stamps are typically organized (although format varies from publisher to publisher) by type of stamp. Definitives and commemoratives are usually—but not always—grouped together followed by semi-postals, airmails, special deliveries, postage dues, officials, and so forth. Each stamp is assigned a unique number known as a catalogue number. Catalogue numbers are the shorthand of the hobby. Mention that you'd like to trade a used U.S. Scott No. 292 for a used Austria Scott No. 380 and the other party, whether in America or somewhere else in the world, will know precisely which two stamps you mean.

This stamp is known as Scott No. 292, Krause-Minkus No. CM24, and Michel No. 124.

Each catalogue publisher uses its own numbering system, so collectors mention both publisher and the number, such as Scott No. 292, which is Krause-Minkus No. CM24, or Michel No. 124, all of which refer to the same stamp. The use of Scott catalogues is so widespread in the United States that catalogue numbers are understood to be Scott numbers unless otherwise indicated.

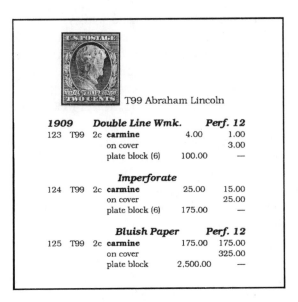

T99 Abraham Lincoln

1909			Double Line Wmk.		Perf. 12
123	T99	2c	**carmine**	4.00	1.00
			on cover		3.00
			plate block (6)	100.00	—
			Imperforate		
124	T99	2c	**carmine**	25.00	15.00
			on cover		25.00
			plate block (6)	175.00	—
			Bluish Paper		Perf. 12
125	T99	2c	**carmine**	175.00	175.00
			on cover		325.00
			plate block	2,500.00	—

Typical catalogue listing. Note the design identifying number T99.

In addition to a catalogue number, each listing has an illustration, a design identifying number (or letters), description (denomination, color and/or subject), gauge of perforation, watermark (if any), method of printing (engraved, lithographed, etc.), date of issue, color of overprint or surcharge (if any), and a price for mint and used copies. Prices for plate blocks, PNCs, first day covers, and other collectible forms of an issue are listed directly below the main listing. Color shades, varieties, and errors are sublisted (usually indicated by a lower-case letter) below main listings.

Some catalogues list prices for both mint never-hinged and hinged condition. Prices are typically for a middle-of-the-road grade such as F-VF (and in some cases VF), with grades higher or lower worth more or less, something the user must factor on a case by case basis. Make sure you know which grade the listed price refers to when checking on a stamp's price. More about price in the chapter "Condition and Grading."

Many stamps are identical in appearance, but differ in watermark, perforation, or paper, hence the need for design identifying numbers. The two-cent Lincoln design illustrated above is identical on the three listed varieties, yet each is considered a distinct collectible variety, and each has its own separate catalogue number (No. 123 through No. 125 in this hypothetical example). They all share the same design identifying number (T99 in this hypothetical example). They range in value from a dollar to more than a hundred dollars. In this example, the three varieties appear grouped together; however, in some cases varieties do not appear together, so you must check throughout the listings to locate all the possible varieties. For the most part, this isn't as confusing as it sounds. Only a few stamps are as complex as the two-cent Lincoln. The vast majority consist of a single variety and have only one catalogue number. Still, pay careful attention to all a stamp's elements, not just its design, when using a catalogue to identify a stamp.

The second function of a stamp catalogue is pricing. The intricacies of pricing are the most confusing, least understood element of stamp catalogues. Just remember, catalogues are general guides to pricing, not the final word on it, for a couple of reasons.

First, catalogues attempt to reflect actual market prices; they do not determine them. Supply and demand determine market prices. The financial section of your daily newspaper reports the prices of stocks; it does not determine them. Stamp catalogues perform the same function, except that they're published only once a year, rather than daily. During the course of a year, the stamp market moves according to its own rhythm, responding to a variety of factors, such as the state of the economy, supply and demand in foreign markets, and exchange rates. Many kinds of things can affect pricing between the publication of one edition of a catalogue and the next. For the most part, however, stamp prices are not volatile and catalogue prices remain reasonably reliable; nevertheless, always remember that the market is the final arbiter of price. Advertisements in philatelic publications are a good way to keep up-to-date on actual prices.

Second, unlike stocks, stamps vary physically from one another (condition), and like gemstones, they are priced on their individual merits. Stamp retail prices are usually quoted in terms of discounts (or premiums) from catalogue that take into account a stamp's individual condition. For example, a severely impaired mint copy of the U.S. $1 Cattle in the Storm commemorative might retail for as little as $150, while a superb, never-hinged copy can easily cost thousands of dollars. Hundreds of combinations and permutations of condition are possible. Just remember, each stamp is priced according to its merits.

Actual market values for early nineteenth-century stamps often vary greatly from catalogue prices because most examples are faulty—and priced as such—while catalogue prices are for sound stamps. Catalogues clearly state in their introductions that catalogue prices are for sound stamps, yet catalogue users routinely overlook or ignore this fact. So, often the joy of discovering that the catalogue value of your Bavarian States stamps is $1,000, is replaced by shock and disbelief when learning that they're really worth only $50 because they're faulty. This because there is little market for damaged stamps; serious collectors want sound examples. The only way dealers can move damaged stamps is to discount them to the bone. Remember, catalogue prices are high for *sound* nineteenth-century stamps not because they are rare, *but because they are rare in sound condition.*

Market price varies from catalogue price for another reason. Heretofore, we've talked about stamps of measurable individual value. On the other hand, thousands of stamps exist with no measurable individual value. Flag definitives on incoming mail are basically worthless. No one ever buys one from a dealer. Collectors soak them off letters or obtain them from mixtures that sell by the pound. Still, regardless of how common it is, every stamp has a minimum catalogue value—typically fifteen cents—to cover a dealer's time and overhead for stocking and delivering it on demand, should someone request it. Think of minimum catalogue value as a service charge.

In summary, stamp catalogues are the key reference tool for the hobby. Technical information, such as the kind used to describe and identify stamps, remains constant; prices fluctuate over time. Market prices may be higher of lower than catalogue prices. Condition is the primary factor in pricing.

WHERE TO GET STAMPS
and Other Resources

PERSONAL SOURCES

A fresh supply of stamps arrives every day on incoming household and business mail. Much of it is collectible and some of it even has cash value. Dealers often pay $1 to $4 per stamp for sound, device-cancelled (as opposed to pen-cancelled) copies of priority mail and express mail stamps (no postage meter imprints, please). They won't buy damaged copies, and they pay very little for pen-cancelled copies. A word of advice, leave stamps on cover until you have enough experience to know which ones can safely be removed.

PNC collectors love finding examples on cover, and junk mail offers a never-ending supply. Examine coil stamps on cover for the tiny plate numbers that appear every so often at the bottom of stamps. You won't find many, but when you find one, leave the cover intact.

Look for dollar-denomination stamps ($1 denominations and up) on cover, interesting usages such as registered and certified mail, and errors stamps. (More about errors in "Errors on Stamps.") Again, leave covers intact until you have enough experience to know which stamps can be removed without impairing their value.

Travel agencies often receive an abundance of foreign mail. Ask them to save covers intact for you. Ask friends, neighbors, and relatives to save covers for you and to check their attics, trunks, and basements for old letters or stamps. Businesses, state agencies, even historical societies often discard outdated correspondence (including covers), some of it going back more than a century. These make fertile hunting grounds. Keep an eye open for anything unusual—civil war covers (especially covers with patriotic cachets, POW covers, and anything with Confederate stamps), pony express covers, local posts, high denominations, out-of-the-ordinary markings (e.g., "Via Aeroplane" or "Censored"), runs of correspondence from western settlers (especially with manuscript or fort postmarks), and anything of historical significance relating to an event or personality. Modern mail also offers opportunities. Keep your eyes open for cover from domestic Japanese internment camps during World War II, illustrated V-mail, POW mail (both U.S. or foreign), and covers from Vietnam, just to mention a few. As you learn more about philately and postal history, you'll better understand what to look for.

Often you'll find stamps at flea markets and estate sales. A word of caution—flea market operators sometimes buy unwanted remainders from stamp dealers and offer them for resale at prices higher than one would otherwise pay at a stamp dealer. These kinds of operators prefer old, intriguing-looking albums that look as if they might be valuable just because they're old. But remember, being old doesn't automatically mean that a stamp is valuable. Before taking a flyer, it's best to gain a little experience. The word of caution notwithstanding, treasures wait to be found at flea markets and estate sales. Some of the most profitable are correspondences that appear innocuous to the untrained eye but are valuable by virtue of esoteric markings, origins, or destinations. The key is knowledge, which enables you to recognize opportunity when it presents itself. The more philatelic knowledge you have, the better your odds of finding treasure.

It's not uncommon to discover an enclosure in a cover—and the tales they tell range from the mundane to the heartstopping: flood, famine, Indian attacks, disease—and none of it filtered through the eyes of an historian. Few things can match the thrill of holding in one's hand an actual bit of history, for as you read the writer's words you cannot help but wonder, who were these people and what were their lives really like? And therein lies the fun.

POST OFFICES

The most obvious place to buy stamps is the post office. Most large cities (and many smaller ones) have philatelic centers that cater to stamp collectors. Philatelic centers usually stock a wide assortment of issues, many of which are not always available at regular windows. Clerks at philatelic centers usually have information on local clubs and upcoming shows, and they know who the local dealers are. You can also order stamps directly from the USPS Philatelic Fulfillment Service Center in Kansas City. Check the Resource Guide for the address.

U.S. Postal Service philatelic window.

Virtually every nation in the world maintains a philatelic agency from which collectors can order new and recent issues at face value. In addition, some foreign postal administrations have agencies in the United States from which collectors can obtain stamps at face value without having to send abroad. Most offer a standing order service that allows you to receive new issues automatically against a deposit.

LOCAL DEALERS

Local dealers usually stock singles, sets, covers, mixtures, packets, accumulations, remainders—just about anything philatelic. Explain that you're just getting started, and don't be afraid to ask questions. Most dealers are eager to help and generous with their knowledge.

Most experienced collectors have had a dealer mentor, one who helped them get started, one upon whom they could rely for advice, one who would keep an eye open for stamps to meet their specific needs as they became more advanced.

Dealers network; they maintain contacts all over the country, and often in foreign countries. If they don't have an item, they can usually obtain it for you or tell you where to find it. Shopping at a local dealer enables you to see stamps before buying, and to compare different types of albums, mounts, and supplies. And a good dealer is tuned into everything philatelic going on in his or her area—meetings, clubs, shows, etc. Shopping at a local dealer also provides the opportunity to meet other collectors.

Sooner or later, you'll find one dealer who's been more helpful than the others, who you enjoy talking to, and who seems to have just the right stamps for you. He's an invaluable resource. Check the Yellow Pages for dealers in your area.

DIRECT MAIL

Advertisements and Pricelists. The more you learn about stamps, the more you'll discover that philately is largely an enterprise of specialists, both dealers and collectors. A single dealer—even the largest—can't stock everything, either stamps or supplies. Fortunately, you can order just about anything by mail: individual stamps, sets, mixtures, job lots, covers, supplies, books, new issues, you name it. Some dealers offer a selective new issue service for topical collectors interested in obtaining only newly issued stamps relating to their topic. Many dealers will send price lists upon request. Philatelic periodicals contain hundreds of dealer display ads and classified ads. Most direct mail dealers are members of the American Philatelic Society (APS) or the American Stamp Dealers Association (ASDA) and subscribe to those organizations' codes of ethics.

Approvals. The term "approvals" refers to selections of stamps sent by mail for purchase, subject to the buyer's approval. You look a selection over (the time allotted is usually 10 to 15 days),

A typical approval selection.

pay for those you keep (there is no obligation to keep any), and return the rest. An initial selection usually amounts to ten dollars or less. The value of subsequent selections increases as you establish creditworthiness. Most approval dealers offer a discount if you purchase the entire selection. In addition, some approval dealers allow you to earn credits (similar to frequent flier miles) toward future purchases. The first selection includes a questionnaire on which to indicate collecting preferences, so that future selections can be oriented toward your interests. You'll continue to receive additional selections automatically until you notify the approval company to stop sending them. The mention of approvals almost invariably brings a smile of fond recollection to even the most seasoned philatelist's face. Countless numbers of collectors have been introduced to the hobby through approvals. Philatelic periodicals contain advertisements for approval dealers.

Trading. Check the classified section of philatelic periodicals for collectors interested in trading. Trading for cheap stamps is usually based on a stamp for stamp basis; new issues on a face-value-for-face-value basis; and expensive, older stamps on a catalogue-value-for-catalogue-value basis. Any equitable, mutually agreeable basis is okay. Many collectors enjoy the personal, one-on-one interaction with trading partners, especially those in foreign countries. You'd be surprised how many foreigners are interested in obtaining U.S. stamps, especially collectors in areas formerly behind the Iron Curtain.

Mass-marketed Philatelic Collectibles. As a rule, collectors rarely recoup their investment from mass-marketed, direct-mail, philatelic collectibles—the type dripping with sugary buzz words such as "officially authorized," "limited edition," and "certificate of authenticity"—and often get no more than a small fraction of the original purchase price when selling. The reason is that no secondary market exists for these products, and stamp dealers won't spend money for inventory that doesn't sell. Stamp collectors prefer real stamps, not contrived collectibles. That's not an aesthetic or moral judgement, just a financial fact. Ask a dealer or fellow collector what has merit and you'll quickly learn what to avoid.

Another caveat: be suspicious of unsolicited direct-mail investment offers promising huge gains in a short period of time. In some cases "investors" receive off-quality stamps at inflated prices In other cases investors are made privy to "inside information" about an issue the "advisors" are promoting. Investors are told that when made public, the inside information will cause the "hot property" to double or triple in short order. Trouble is, real stamp collectors couldn't care less about the "hot property," and when the so-called inside information becomes public, it usually elicits a yawn from the philatelic community rather than a wave of excitement. Before buying any stamp for investment, check with experienced collectors and dealers to find out if a secondary market for it exists.

AUCTION
Stamp auctions are an excellent source of material ranging from scarce individual stamps to collection remainders and bulk lots. Stamp auctions range from small, local, club affairs to multi-million dollar operations. Regardless of their size, the idea is the same: to sell lots to the highest bidder. All stamp auctions publish catalogues containing descriptions, including catalogue number, condition, and price (either catalogue price, estimated cash value, or reserve price). Except in the case of a reserve price, bidders are

Pages from an auction catalogue.

free to bid as much or as little as they please. Most auction catalogues are illustrated, some with photographs of every lot, but most often only the best or most valuable lots. If you attend an auction in person, you can view the lots prior to the start of the sale. Check philatelic periodicals for announcements of forthcoming auctions.

You can bid in person, by mail, or through an agent. Floor bidders (in-person bidders) use a variety of strategies, which are too numerous to go into here. You'll quickly pick up on them if you decide to attend auctions. One strategy, however, is worth mentioning. Experienced bidders follow it religiously: establish your maximum bid for each lot in advance and don't waver from it. The greatest mistake newcomers make is to fantasize about how little they expect to pay for a lot rather than fix a maximum price for it. Then they get caught up in the frenzy of bidding and end up paying more than they should have. Establish your limit in advance. When you hit the limit, drop out. No exceptions. There will always be more stamps. Regular bidders often review prices realized to get an idea of bidding levels for the kinds of stamps they are interested in. Most auctions published prices realized after each sale.

Most auctions add a ten percent (in some cases fifteen percent) buyer's fee to lots at settlement, so factor that into your maximum bid. A few do not charge a buyer's fee, but they're the exception rather than the rule.

Read carefully the terms and conditions in each auction catalogue before bidding. They're highly specific, and vary from auction to auction. All state that placing a bid constitutes a contract. If your bid's successful, you've bought the lot, and lots are generally not returnable (except for cause). You may, at the time of sale, request that a lot be submitted for an expert certificate, in which case the transaction will not be final until the certificate comes back, usually in six to eight weeks. You will be required to make payment for the lot, which the auctioneer will hold pending the outcome of the expert opinion. If the stamp or cover comes back with a good certificate (genuine and as described), you've bought the lot. If the stamp or cover comes back with a bad certificate (not genuine or not as described), the auctioneer returns it to the consignor and refunds your money. It is customary for the auctioneer to pay the cost of a bad certificate, and for the buyer to pay the cost of a good certificate.

You may bid by mail of fax using the bid sheet contained in the auction catalogue. New bidders are required to provide references (society memberships or stamp dealer/financial references), and are usually asked to put down a good faith deposit, typically 25 percent of the sum of the bids. Most auctions—but not all—buy lots for mail bidders at one bid over the highest floor bid, using a mail bidder's maximum bid only if necessary. Most auctions allow "either/or" bidding, which means you can bid on several similar lots but buy only one. Most auctions allow you to place a maximum on the total amount you want to spend. Once you've reached your maximum, the auctioneer stops executing your bids. Most bid sheets contain a box, which when checked, authorizes the auction house to increase your bids by a stated percentage, typically 10 percent or 20 percent. Avoid this. Let your basic bid stand as your maximum bid.

CAUTION: Check your bid sheet carefully before mailing it or faxing it to make sure the lot numbers and bids listed are correct. If you intend to bid $100 on Lot No. 454, but write Lot No. 545 by mistake, you'll be held to it. It won't do any good to argue about it. And if you choose not to honor the bid, forget about bidding anywhere else. Dealers share deadbeat information.

Dealers and sharpshooters (individuals who attend auctions for no other purpose than to pick off bargains) most auctions. They provide the floor beneath which prices do not fall. If you're lucky, you can sometimes purchase a lot for one bid over a dealer's bid (think of it as cost plus). But don't expect to get a rare or superb stamp cheaply. They routinely sell for multiples of catalogue or estimated cash value.

The idea of bidding at auction intimidates many newcomers. To gain a little experience, bid on a few inexpensive lots in a local stamp club auction or small mail bid sale.

TIP: Pros usually avoid bidding on the first of several similar lots. The most eager bidder usually buys the first one, and the price of successive identical lots usually falls as each buyer in turn obtains a lot.

Mail bid sales are similar to auctions except that bidding is done exclusively by mail without an auctioneer or live floor. Mail bid sales differ from auctions in one important respect: expect to pay the full amount of your bid (rather than one increment over the next highest bid), unless the terms and conditions indicate otherwise. So carefully consider your maximum bid on each lot. Mail bid sales usually do not charge a buyer's fee, which simplifies bidding.

STAMP CLUBS

Most stamp clubs permit members to bring stamps to meetings to trade or sell. Stamp clubs also provide a means of networking with fellow collectors and tapping into the tremendous pool of knowledge and experience they possess.

Clubs typically meet once or twice a month. Large metropolitan areas often support several clubs, and collectors who just can't get enough of stamps belong to as many as they have time and energy for. Dues are usually nominal, only a few dollars a year. Ask a local dealer to put you in touch with club representatives. Also, the American Philatelic Society provides its members with a handbook that lists more than 750 local clubs across America. Check the Resource Guide for APS's address.

Some clubs meet in members' homes, but most use church, school, or other public meeting rooms. Meetings often begin with a short business meeting (announcements, discussion of dues, etc., usually no longer than ten or fifteen minutes) followed by a program or slide show presented by a member or guest speaker. The program is usually followed by a general session in which members discuss stamps, compare collections, catch up on the latest news, and buy, sell and trade stamps. Clubs often hold auctions, with a portion (or sometimes all) of the proceeds going to the club treasury, typically to purchase catalogues or benefit members in some other way.

No matter what your level of experience, membership in a local club will increase your knowledge of stamps and enrich your enjoyment of the hobby.

PHILATELIC SOCIETIES

Many philatelic societies make stamps available to members through sales divisions. Philatelic societies—as opposed to stamp clubs—tend to be national in scope, drawing membership from all parts of the country. Rather than frequent meetings, societies tend to hold annual conventions—usually in conjunction with a stamp show—which rotate from city to city. Societies tend to be highly specialized in nature, such as the American First Day Cover Society (AFDCS) or the American Topical Association (ATA). The exception is the American Philatelic Society, which is a general organization.

The APS has so much to offer that it is worth discussing in detail. The APS is a non-profit organization founded in 1886, whose membership stands at about 55,000. The value of APS membership lies in the abundance of resources it puts at members' fingertips. The APS publishes an illustrated, slick-paper monthly journal, the *American Philatelist*, which alone is worth the society's nominal annual dues. Members also receive a services handbook, a dealer directory, and are entitled to a discount on books published by the APS. And the APS offers a stamp insurance plan designed specifically for collectors, one that is less costly and more comprehensive than those available from standard casualty companies.

Upon request, members may obtain circuit books by mail from the APS sales division. Circuit books (they're actually booklets) contain selections of stamps for sale by other members. Members wishing to sell stamps obtain empty circuit books from the APS sales division, fill them and return them to the sales division, which checks the stamps for accuracy and pricing, then enters the books into their inventory for dispatch to member requestees. Recipients make selections (they may purchase as many or as few items as they wish), send payment to APS, and forward the books to the next collector on the list enclosed with the selection—hence the name circuit books. The last collector on the circuit returns the books to the APS. Each recipient pays the cost of postage to forward the books to the next member on the circuit. Circuit books provide access to a wide range of reasonably priced stamps. The service is especially useful to collectors living far from dealers.

APS members are entitled to borrow books from the American Philatelic Research Library (APRL), one of the largest libraries in the world specifically dedicated to philately. The APRL contains two linear miles of shelf space housing tens of thousands of books and periodicals devoted to philately. Most of its book loans are made by mail to members all over America. For those living nearby, the library is located at 100 Oakwood Avenue in State College, Pennsylvania, and is open to the public.

APS members are also entitled to use the services of the American Philatelic Expertizing Service. (More about expertizing in the chapter "Fakes and Forgeries.") While anyone may submit stamps to the American Philatelic Expertizing Service, only APS members receive a discount.

Dozens of other societies exist, one for nearly every specialty, and far too numerous to discuss individually here. Some are large, others small. Most publish journals or newsletters, the size, frequency, and production values of which vary according to the size and budget of the organization. Many publish quarterly; a few more often. Dues are usually nominal. Some offer circuit books, others do not. There is no better way to keep abreast of the latest developments within a specialty than membership in a specialist society.

In summary, philatelic societies offer access to stamps, highly detailed publications, and a network of kindred spirits, whose reservoir of knowledge is both broad and deep.

STAMP SHOWS

Stamp shows generally consist of two elements: a dealer bourse and an exhibition of stamps. Shows range in size from small local affairs with half a dozen dealers to national and international shows featuring hundreds of frames of exhibits and hundreds of dealers.

Collectors browsing at a stamp show bourse.

The bourse section of a show consists of dealers offering their wares from tables or booths. The larger the show, the more dealers. Dealers from all over the world take booths at giant international shows. Stamp shows, regardless of their size, concentrate dealers into a single location, affording the opportunity to view and buy a range of material otherwise unavailable in one place. There's no better place to comparison shop.

One of the most popular attractions at national and international shows is the section of foreign post office booths offering their latest stamps at face value. Some even premier new stamps at shows and have stamp designers available to autograph first day covers.

Local shows are usually held annually, although it's not uncommon for a large metropolitan area to host a number of shows sponsored by different groups during the course of a year. Dealer bourses (usually one-day affairs without exhibits) are common in large cities, and are typically held once or twice a month.

The exhibition section of a show features exhibits prepared by collectors and displayed in rows of large frames. The U.S. Postal Service sometimes displays an exhibit of proofs, uncut press sheets, and other material from its archives that's seldom available for viewing by the public. On occasion, the Bureau of Engraving and Printing brings a small intaglio press (known as a spider press) and demonstrates the intaglio printing process by hand printing souvenir cards, which visitors may buy. Attending a national or international show is like going to Disneyland. You leave disappointed that you had not allowed more time to see and do things.

Exhibits are especially worthwhile for the novice. Nothing gives one a better feel for philately than viewing exhibits and seeing how others have approached collecting. In addition, large shows often feature lectures, programs, and seminars, usually at no cost, which are valuable learning tools. There is no better place to meet fellow collectors, ask questions, share information, view and learn.

INTERNET

The Internet is a tremendous resource, too vast to even attempt to cover in detail. We will only touch on the basics, trusting that through the power of search engines and the cross-pollination of interlinks, you will have no trouble discovering hundreds of philatelic websites.

The Internet has opened up the possibility of buying, selling, and trading directly with other individual collectors all over the world. In addition, you can purchase stamps and supplies directly from dealers, many of whom participate in electronic malls, such as Zillions of Stamps (*www.zillionsofstamps.com*) hosted by *Linn's Stamp News*, and by StampFinder (*www.stampfinder.com*), which offers classified ads, a want list service, an events calendar, hundreds of philatelic links, and an Internet magazine, *Stamps.Net* (*www.stamps.net*).

Online auctions fall into two categories: party-to-party auctions and traditional auctions. Party-to-party auction sites act at arm's length, offering only a forum in which buyer and seller interact directly. Ebay (*www.ebay.com*) is one of the largest, although not devoted exclusively to stamps. Countless others exist and new ones seem to spring up all the time. AuctionWatch (*www.auctionwatch.com*) offers a universal search feature that, in essence, serves as a link to all Internet auctions.

More and more traditional auctions, too, are going online. They differ from party-to-party auctions in that they actually receive the stamps to be sold, examine them, and verify them. This gives bidders an added level of comfort in knowing that lots are accurately described and graded, which is especially important when dealing with expensive stamps. In addition, numerous other auctions offer their services through stand-alone websites.

Check out the APS website (*www.stamps.org*). It contains too much to describe in detail here, but will get you on your way in philatelic cyberspace. Also pay a visit to the American Philatelic Research Library (APRL) site (through the APS website) for the most comprehensive resource in existence devoted to philatelic literature. Its card catalogue and article index are truly mind-boggling.

Youngsters will want to check out the Junior Philatelists of America (JPA) website (*www.jpastamps.org*), which offers help for beginners, contests and games, and more. The JPA is a non-profit organization devoted to youth philately.

You will also find a variety of useful software on the market, including database programs for maintaining an inventory of your collection and creating want lists. Most contain catalogue prices and offer annual pricing upgrades. Some allow you to store images of your own stamps. You can also design your own album pages with software and print them on any paper you wish, a welcome feature for those who prefer archival paper. Individual sources are listed in the Bibliography, along with Universal Resource Locators (URLs) where known.

GETTING STARTED

One of the easiest ways to get your feet wet is with a starter kit. There are several on the market, all reasonably priced. Each contains the essentials: an assortment of stamps (usually 100 or 200), a basic album, a pair of tongs, a perforation gauge, a magnifying glass, hinges, and an informational booklet. Or you can buy the individual items separately.

The best way to become familiar with stamps is to handle them. In doing so, you will acquire the basic skills you'll use throughout your collecting life. And in the beginning, work with as many different kinds of stamps as possible. You will learn much about the hobby this way. Most advanced collectors started out as generalists with packets and mixtures spread out on the kitchen table.

MIXTURES AND PACKETS

Mixtures and packets are perhaps the most economical way of obtaining a great variety of stamps. Mixtures contain an assortment of stamps—usually including a fair number of duplicates—and are therefore, less expensive than packets. Mixtures come in two forms: on paper and off paper. Off-paper mixtures are more expensive than on-paper mixtures because of the cost of removing them from paper. Mixtures come in many varieties, from general worldwide to those containing stamps of a single country or type, such as pictorials or high values. Mixtures rich in pictorials are more expensive than those containing all types of stamps, including run-of-the-mill definitives—which are the majority found on every day on mail. Some collectors prefer off-paper mixtures because they require no soaking and are ready to mount. Others prefer on-paper mixtures because they get more stamps for their money and because they regard soaking as fun rather than work.

Packets differ from mixtures in that they usually contain all-different stamps, which means no duplicates. Stamps in packets are off paper and ready to mount. Packets range from general worldwide to specific countries or topics, such as 100 different Germany or 500 different butterfly stamps. Prices of packets vary according to the kind and quality of stamps they contain: mint or used, pictorial or definitive, and so forth.

Mixtures are usually sold by weight—by the ounce, pound, or kilogram. Packets are usually sold by count and range in size from as few as ten different to as many as 50,000 different. Small packets (under 500 stamps) contain the most common stamps and are, therefore, the most economical. Large packets are usually more costly on a per-stamp basis because they include better items, which are necessary in order to make the selection all-different. Still, buying packets is less expensive than buying stamps one at a time. A selection of packets or a pound or two of mixture containing a couple thousand stamps is more than enough to get you started.

APPROVALS

Many collectors build their collections with approvals, especially those who live far from a stamp dealer. Approval dealers range in size from multi-million dollar companies to mom-and-pop operations. Large ones offer a great variety of stamps; small ones, more personal service and selections custom tailored to exact individual tastes and budgets.

SOAKING STAMPS

Stamps are soaked to remove them from their backing paper. Soaking stamps is one of the fundamental skills worth mastering even if you don't make a habit of processing pounds of mixture. Even the most advanced collector occasionally comes across a special stamp that needs to be removed from paper before it can be mounted. And when that happens, he or she will rely on their basic soaking skill to remove the stamp safely and without damage.

In its basic form, soaking consists of little more than immersing stamps in water, waiting for them to separate from their backing paper, then rinsing and drying them.

The first step is to immerse the stamps in water. A medium-size bowl works well. Start with a few stamps, perhaps two or three dozen. Don't try to soak too many at once, especially in the beginning. Wait until you have a firm grasp of the process before trying to do a sinkful at one time.

Fill the bowl about three-quarters full with cool or lukewarm water. Stamps separate from paper more slowly in cold water; hot water tends to make stamp paper pulpy and fragile. Hot water also accelerates the bleeding of certain types of cancellations, especially red or magenta.

CAUTION: Avoid soaking stamps on colored paper such as the kind used for Christmas card envelopes. It is especially prone to bleeding. One piece can discolor and ruin a whole batch of soaked stamps.

Stamps will start to float free in about ten to fifteen minutes. Don't be impatient and attempt to hasten the process by pulling stamps from their backing. Wet paper is fragile and easily damaged. Tugging at stamps sometimes causes the printed image on some modern issues to crack, so let stamps float free of their own accord. As the stamps float free, remove the bits of backing paper from the bowl until only the stamps remain. Test a few stamps between your thumb and forefinger to make sure all the gum is dissolved; if it's not, it will adhere to the drying medium and you'll have to re-soak them. Postal services use a variety of gums on modern stamps, and their solubility varies from stamp to stamp. Some require longer immersion in water than others. If the back of the stamp feels slick, it is not free of gum. You may try to hasten its removal by gently sliding your thumb over the gum, but never use too much pressure or you may end up taking off part of the stamp itself. Some collectors separate stamps with slow-to-dissolve gum into a separate bowl for additional soaking time. Experiment on some inexpensive examples and see what works best for you.

Next, carefully drain the water from the bowl and run additional lukewarm water in to rinse the stamps. This will flush away any dissolved gum and leave the stamps cleaner.

Now you're ready to dry your stamps. Stamps are usually dried by layering them between sheets of paper or blotter and adding weight on top to press them. Collectors have used everything from newsprint to old telephone books to dry stamps, but blotters work best because they avoid the possibility of smudging or offset from printing inks. White blotters (never use colored blotters) of the type used by photographers work best. Desk blotters usually contain a pattern, which often ends up impressed on stamps. Photographers' blotters contain no pattern and come in large sheets that can be cut into a convenient size to fit beneath whatever weight you intend to use for pressing. Or, you can purchase a stamp-drying book, which is nothing more than several sheets of blotter paper bound together.

Some collectors place stamps directly from the soaking bowl onto the drying medium. Others lay wet stamps on paper towels first to absorb excess moisture. This because the less moisture a stamp contains before being pressed, the more quickly it will dry. In any case, place stamps face down on the drying medium. Wet stamps tend to curl toward the face side; placing them face down helps keep them from curling while you're arranging them. One of the advantages of blotters over drying books is that you can

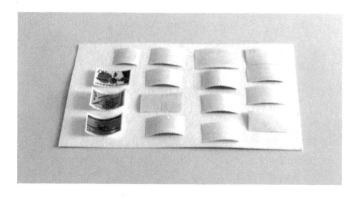

Stamps laid out on a blotter; notice the tendency to curl.

leave each layer open to the air while arranging other layers, stacking the layers only when the last is finished. Pre-blotting and exposing layers to open air before stacking shortens drying time. Don't worry about stamps getting too dry before pressing. Even once they begin to look a little wrinkly, they'll still press out nicely under a weight. When you've finished laying out the stamps, stack the layers and place them under a weight sufficient to press them flat. Books work well, but any heavy object will do. One collector uses cinder blocks because they are both heavy and porous, allowing a stack of blotters to dry rapidly. Stack the layers carefully, checking to make sure none of the stamps are curled to the point of being bent or creased when placed under weight. Corners of stamps are especially prone to inadvertent creasing.

TIP: Don't pile too many blotters in one stack or they will tend to warp and buckle, even under weight. A dozen layers in any one stack is usually the maximum.

Depending on the time of year and the humidity of your climate, drying can take anywhere from a few hours to several days. The fellow who uses cinder blocks lives in the Southwest. He puts a stack of blotters under a of couple cinder blocks on his patio in the summer and reports that the stack takes only a couple of hours to dry in the sun. Drying time in mid-winter Seattle will, of course, be longer.

A stamp press is ideal for pressing small batches of stamps.

When your stamps are dry, remove them carefully from the blotters and mount them in your album. You may find that some have adhered to the blotter and require resoaking. The type most likely to adhere to a blotter are those possessing "dry" or "flat" PVA (polyvinyl alcohol) gum, which the postal service began usingon some stamps in the late 1970s. It's so insoluble that no amount of soaking seems to completely remove it. Experienced collectors let PVA-gummed stamps air dry almost completely—about 95 percent—then press them in small batches on perfectly dry blotter paper. In this fashion, they will usually press out without sticking to the blotter. A small stamp press is useful for drying small batches of stamps such as these. They're available from stamp dealers and mail order supply firms.

Gum on modern U.S. self-adhesive stamps is water soluble, but dissolves at a slower rate than gum on "lick-and-stick" stamps, so handling then requires a little practice. Practice soaking some self-adhesive stamps that arrive on your incoming mail. Also, be aware that the self-adhesive on stamps issued before 1990 (such as the U.S. Christmas stamp of 1975) is usually not water soluble, and attempting to soak them in water will ruin them. When in doubt, consult a stamp catalogue, stamp dealer, or fellow collector before soaking the item in question.

SORTING

Some collectors prefer to sort stamps before soaking, leaving those for which they have no immediate use on paper. Others prefer to soak an entire mixture before sorting. Either way, spread your mixture out on a work area large enough to accommodate a number of sorting piles. Kitchen tables often turn out to be the surface of choice. Begin sorting by putting like stamps together. Worldwide mixtures are usually first rough sorted by country, then countries sorted by series or similar designs, then by denomination. As you sort, you'll see that some stamps seem to belong together and fall into natural groupings. Often, they're part of a set and fit together on an album page.

From each group of identical stamps select the most visually pleasing example to mount. Look for balanced centering and a light, unobtrusive postmark. Sometimes, you'll have no choice other than a poor example. Mount it anyway; replace it later when a better copy comes along. This is known as upgrading.

Store duplicates in glassine envelopes or on stock sheets. Glassines are especially useful when dealing with a large number of duplicates. Glassines come in a variety of sizes, hold a lot of stamps, allow you to see what's inside, and store conveniently in boxes. Stock sheets are handier for trading sessions because they allow stamps to be easily viewed and removed.

Duplicates can be used for trading or making packets. Often, local dealers will take packets made by collectors, either paying cash or allowing credit toward purchases. Some collectors use a combination of methods: stock sheets for stamps to be mounted or interesting duplicates (such as those with unusual postmarks) and glassines for everything else. There are many ways of organizing duplicates. With a little experimentation, you'll find a system that works best for you.

IDENTIFYING

Most stamps are fairly easy to identify; however, in any group of foreign stamps, you'll encounter some whose country of origin is not immediately recognizable. Check these in your stamp identification guide. As you use the identification guide, you'll be amazed at how quickly you learn to recognize exotic names and phrases on stamps, and before long, few items will stump you.

And as you work with stamps, you'll quickly become familiar with styles of various countries and eras. These characteristics will often be enough to enable you to recognize where a stamp belongs

The stamp on the left is from Japan; the one on the right from Greece.

without any further investigation. Illustrations in album spaces, too, aid in identification. As you work with your album, you'll become familiar with stamps of various countries just from seeing their illustrations time and time again.

Inevitably, you'll end up with a few stamps that defy all attempts at identification. Put them aside and show them to a more experienced collector or stamp dealer. They'll usually have the answer.

MOUNTING

Once you have sorted and identified a batch of stamps, you're ready to mount them. Find the album space identical to the stamp and place it there. Pay attention to overprints and other differences (often subtle) that indicate a stamp may belong elsewhere. Many stamps are identical except for denomination, so take a moment to be sure you're mounting the stamp in the right space. Many general albums illustrate only the lowest few denominations in a set or series, leaving blank spaces for higher values. Arrange stamps for which no illustrations appear on blank spaces near those of similar design or where you feel they may logically fit. Mount these in ascending order by denomination.

Sometimes you won't find an illustration for a stamp because you're looking in the wrong country. Check your identification guide to make sure the stamp is actually from the country you think it's from. In some cases, you won't find a space for a stamp because it was issued after your album was printed. Check a stamp catalogue to verify when it was issued. If it was issued later than your album was printed, mount it on a blank page following the illustrated stamps. In some cases, you won't find an illustration because the stamp is scarce and infrequently encountered. These stamps, too, can be mounted on blank spaces.

TIP: New catalogues are expensive. Beginners often buy a used two- or three-year-old catalogue. Most dealers sell them for a few dollars, and they are just as useful for stamp identification as a current edition.

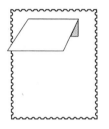

Most beginners use hinges to mount stamps because they're economical and easy to use. Hinges are best for used stamps, cancelled-to-order stamps, or mint stamps of nominal value. Be sparing when applying moisture to hinges. Too much moisture warps the stamp, warps the album paper, and leaves a bigger hinge mark later when it is removed.

Also, do not attempt to remove a freshly applied hinge from a stamp. Wait until the hinge is thoroughly dry before pulling it off, otherwise you may damage the stamp.

Plastic stamp mounts are generally used for mint stamps when the value of preserving their gum in a never-hinged state is greater than the cost of the mounts. It doesn't make sense to spend a dollar for mounts to house fifty cents worth of stamps. On the other hand, it makes sense to spend a dollar to protect a fifty-dollar set, especially if its value falls to thirty dollars when hinged.

CAUTION: Always use a mount large enough to accommodate a stamp comfortably. Never try to force a stamp into a mount too small or too tightly fitting. You'll either damage the stamp right then, or it will warp with the passing of time (plastic and paper expand and contract at different rates). Either way, you will have ruined the stamp. And be careful not to use too much moisture when moistening the back of a mount. Excess moisture will leak onto the gum, defeating the whole purpose of the mount. To avoid this problem, some collectors install mounts on pages before inserting stamps in them. Never mount stamps or covers by taping or gluing them down, and do not use cellophane tape to secure the sides of plastic mounts.

ALBUM

General worldwide albums provide printed spaces for the most frequently encountered stamps—usually inexpensive sets and lower values of expensive sets and series—and blank spaces near the printed spaces for less frequently encountered varieties. General albums usually contain spaces only for face-different stamps, i.e., stamps that differ from one another in appearance rather than by perforation, watermark, or type of paper. When getting started, choose an album or set of albums that looks like it will reasonably accommodate your near-term collecting needs. An inexpensive one- or two-volume worldwide album is usually sufficient to get you started. As mentioned earlier, loose-leaf albums are best because they allow you to add blank pages and supplements.

If general worldwide collecting turns out to be your passion, you can expand to a multi-volume set of albums (the largest contains more than 30 volumes) that contain spaces for virtually every stamp in the world, which number several hundreds of thousands.

If you decide to collect U.S. stamps, you'll find a good selection of inexpensive albums that contain spaces for just about every stamp. Some omit spaces for rarities, such as nineteenth-century reissues, which is okay because you'll not be running across them anyway. You'll also find a variety of top-of-the-line U.S. albums, some costing as much as several hundred dollars. They are printed on higher quality paper, contain fewer spaces per page, and in some cases, contain hingeless mounts. It is wise, however, to start with an inexpensive album and gain experience before committing to an expensive album.

A wide variety of foreign specialty albums exists. Some are published in the United States; others are published abroad. The best among them are expensive—several hundred dollars and up.

Most beginners quickly outgrow their first album, but it will have performed a valuable service. It will have made you aware of the features you would like in your next album. This is important because the next album you choose often ends up lasting a lifetime.

BUILDING YOUR COLLECTION

If you have a local stamp dealer in your area or access to stamp shows, you'll discover counter boxes and "pick-em" books.

Counter boxes contain loose stamps that you can pick through and select from. For years they were known as penny boxes because their contents were priced at one cent each. These days, they're more likely to be priced from two cents to five cents per stamp. Pick-em books are albums from which the premium items have been removed. The remainders are priced per stamp, often five cents and up, depending on the quality of the stamps. An album that started out at a twenty-five cents per stamp will be reduced in price as it's picked over until it ends up a nickel-per-stamp book. Higher priced books generally contain a better grade of stamps. Whatever the price, you page through pick-em books, pulling whatever strikes your eye. The advantage to counter boxes and pick-em books is that you take only what you need, eliminating the possibility of duplication. Stamps in counter boxes and pick-em books are usually more economical than packets because dealers incur no labor cost in preparing them for sale.

After a period of time, you will probably begin to gravitate toward a country or topic that interests you more than others. This is a natural course of events, one that leads to specializing. You'll begin to want to fill out some of the spaces for older, more expensive stamps. And although you may obtain some by trading with other collectors, sooner or later, you'll have to depend on a dealer or bidding at auction to obtain what you need.

At this point, you'll be firmly launched into the world of philately. You will have discovered that every stamp is a work of art, every collection like a miniature art gallery. You will have discovered that every stamp has a story, that learning about these stories heightens your enjoyment of the hobby, and that your satisfaction and delight in this knowledge grows with the passing of time. You'll find that the satisfaction derived in building your collection, too, grows as time passes. You'll come to enjoy each stamp and each set, and find that they remain favorites—even become old friends—with the passing of years. Even after moving on to a specialty, most collectors keep their beginning collection, and even decades later, retain a special fondness for it.

METHODS OF COLLECTING

Most collectors collect according to their budget, which is a good idea. Nothing becomes frustrating more quickly than a goal too financially ambitious. Some collectors prefer colorful stamps, others prefer stamps with a connection to history. Still others enjoy the challenge of locating hard-to-find items. And there are some who find the social interaction with fellow collectors to be the most enjoyable. So, follow your inclinations and remember, there are as many ways of forming a stamp collection as there are human personalities. It all comes down to what you like.

Many collectors enjoy "dressing up" their collections with visually interesting items such as first day covers, maximum cards, postcards, exhibition tickets, photographs, proofs, anything relating to an issue of stamps or events surrounding its issuance. Collateral material (as these stamp-related items are known) adds color to album pages and helps tell the story of the stamps next to which it appears. Some collectors enjoy pursuing collateral material as much as pursuing stamps themselves.

MINT VERSUS USED

Soon after becoming interested in stamps, most collectors tend to gravitate toward either mint stamps or used stamps. Those who prefer mint stamps feel that cancellations intrude on a stamp's design and distract from its beauty, and that soaking a stamp off paper diminishes its freshness. Those who prefer used stamps usually argue that a stamp is not really a stamp until it's gone through the mail, been cancelled, and served its intended purpose. You might as well argue about which is better, chocolate or vanilla. As a practical matter, country collectors usually obtain mint stamps as far back as they can, then fill in with used stamps. The dividing line for United States stamps is usually around the years 1890 or 1900.

GENERAL COLLECTING

There was a time—now long past—when all the different stamps of the world would fit in a single album, and collectors tried to obtain an example of each. They were known as general collectors. Today it requires more than thirty albums, each four to five inches thick, to accommodate all the stamps of the world, which number several hundred thousand. And the annual cost to acquire all the new issues of the world—and there are thousands—is staggering, usually around $7,500.

Today, general collectors rarely collect with an eye toward completion. Instead, they enjoy the challenge of seeing how many different stamps they can acquire. Some buy selectively. Others buy in bulk in the form of job lots, remainders, and cartons full of stamps, searching them for what they can use, then selling the balance to finance subsequent purchases.

A new breed of generalists collect just those sets and singles that catch their eye, stamps that may have no logical relationship to one another, but which they, nevertheless, find intriguing. This form of limited general collecting is becoming more popular all the time. One fellow calls his general collection simply "personal favorites." He houses his stamps on black stock sheets and says he gets as much enjoyment from viewing them as from viewing his more expensive specialized collections.

COUNTRY COLLECTING

Country collecting, i.e., collecting the stamps of a nation, is the most popular method of collecting both here and abroad. Collectors of each nation tend to collect the stamps of their country: Americans collect U.S. stamps; Germans collect German stamps; Chinese collect Chinese stamps. Americans also enjoy collecting foreign stamps, most often from the nations of their ethnic heritage. Images on stamps from our ancestral homelands have a powerful effect; holding the stamps and pondering the images puts us directly in touch with our ethnic history and our roots.

Most country collectors house their collections in specialty albums, which can be purchased from a stamp dealer or mail order supply dealer. A great variety of country albums exist ranging in price from $40 or $50 to many hundreds of dollars, depending on the size of the country's output, the album's degree of comprehensiveness, and the quality of the album.

TOPICAL COLLECTING

Topical collecting is popular because it's simple and so much fun. The idea is to acquire as many different stamps as possible illustrating a topic of interest. Among the more popular topics are dogs, cats, birds, flowers, aircraft, trains, ships, fine art, music, aerospace, sports, and religion. Even Elvis and Marilyn Monroe are collected. The choices are limited only by one's imagination.

A sampling of popular topics.

Topics need not be limited to the subject of a stamp. Czeslaw Slania, one of the world's most talented and prolific stamp engravers, has more than a thousand stamps to his credit, all incredibly detailed, all miniature masterpieces. A growing number of collectors specialize in acquiring just those stamps engraved by this master.

There was once a woman who collected only stamps printed in green. Another fellow limited his collection exclusively to stamps bearing the numeral 10. And at least one collector judiciously acquires stamps that are not really stamps, i.e., pseudo-stamps used in advertising and promotion. He has amassed hundreds of examples, which when displayed together are indeed striking, and evidence of how pervasive, if only subliminally, postage stamps are in our lives and culture.

Washington Press publishes a variety of high-quality pages for topicals under the brand name White Ace. The American Topical Association (ATA), one of the largest philatelic societies in the world, offers much to the topicalist, including their journal the *Topical Time*; a marvelous variety of handbooks devoted to specific topics; and circuit books.

POSTAL HISTORY

Strictly speaking, postal history is the study and collection of stamps, covers, or other materials relating to the operation or evolution of a postal system or element of a postal system. Lately, the term "postal history" is being used more loosely to describe covers that illustrate or relate to some historical epoch, such as World War II. Postal history collections are essentially stories told and illustrated through the use of covers and stamps.

Postal history knows no national boundaries and any facet of the development of the delivery of mail can be collected and studied. For example, the Confederate postal system, the pony express, or the evolution of modern express mail. The most trying times in

A postal history specialist could explain why these U.S. stamps were used in China.

human history often provide the most exciting and fertile ground for the postal history collector.

Postal history can be as expensive or inexpensive as one chooses to make it. It is not uncommon to see valuable and remarkable collections assembled from seemingly unremarkable parts. Knowledge enables the postal history collector to do this. Postal history collectors love to trade stories about the valuable covers they've found in dealers' bargain boxes, covers passed over by others because no one recognized their significance. Finding these treasures is part of the appeal of postal history.

Some contend that every cover tells a story, if only one inquires deeply enough. And it's true. That's what postal history is all about.

OTHERS METHODS OF COLLECTING

Accumulating and Hoarding. Not all stamp collectors are organized or focused. The hobby is home to many "hoarders" and "accumulators" who buy, trade, or otherwise try to get as many stamps as they can. Some are treasure hunters; others just love to accumulate stamps and covers for no particular reason.

Some accumulators buy job lots (large, often disorganized accumulations), remainders, and mixtures from dealers, estates, and auctions hoping to find something valuable that someone else overlooked or didn't have sufficient knowledge to recognize. Others search lots and mixtures, remove what they want, then sell or trade the balance (often for a profit) to offset the cost of what they've kept. Still others bring boxes and cartons home and put them in closets or basements, where they gather dust for years. The dyed-in-the-wool hoarder seems to get more of a kick out of acquiring stamps than doing anything with them.

Some enterprising individuals arrange to get empty envelopes from utility companies or other high-volume mail sources and sift through them looking for oddities and unusual items, which either interest them, fit in their collections, or which they can sell. This low-cost method of collecting requires no special tools except access to raw material, a willingness to sort through it, and a knowledge of what to look for.

Casual Collecting. According to the U.S. Postal Service, many Americans save (rather than collect) stamps; that is to say they tuck away examples of only those stamps that appeal to them, such as those featuring Elvis or Marilyn Monroe. They're neither aware of nor participate in organized philately. They don't own albums, tongs, or accessories. They retain only those stamps they like with no thought of forming a collection. According to the postal service, more than 20 million Americans are casual collectors.

Investing. Investors buy stamps with an eye toward profit (building a portfolio) rather than aesthetics or completion. They often store their acquisitions in a safe deposit box. The book *Stamp Investing* is a must for anyone interested in stamps as investments. Refer to the Bibliography.

UNITED STATES
Collecting U.S. stamps is the most popular specialty in America, and there are so many sub-specialties that they could easily fill a book by themselves. We'll touch on the basics in the next chapter.

In summary, tailor your collection to fit your interests and your budget. Above all, collect what you enjoy. That's what it's is all about.

COLLECTING U.S. STAMPS

Collecting United States stamps is by far the most popular specialty in America. The majority of U.S. collectors approach the hobby in one of several ways: collecting singles, plate blocks, PNCs, first day covers, or specializing in an individual stamp or series.

GENERAL U.S. COLLECTING

Collecting single copies of stamps (as opposed to blocks or panes) is the most economical and least complex way of collecting U.S. stamps. Most collectors try to obtain an example of every U.S. postage stamp ever issued, beginning with the latest stamps available at the post office and working backward, crossing the bridges presented by expensive items as they come to them. Assembling a collection of twentieth-century stamps is not particularly difficult, although it is more costly to collect mint stamps than used stamps. Still, you need not be wealthy to form such a collection.

Collecting nineteenth-century stamps is a different story. Only the most dedicated collector with unlimited funds stands a chance of completing a mint collection of nineteenth-century stamps. It is much less costly and far more realistic to collect used nineteenth-century stamps, which is what most collectors, even serious ones, usually do. Of course, you can fill spaces for less expensive nineteenth-century stamps with mint copies if you choose, and many do. As a practical matter, most U.S. collections contain mint examples of twentieth-century issues and used examples of nineteenth-century issues.

A few collectors limit their scope to commemorative stamps, which pretty much eliminates nineteenth century issues.

TIP: Limit your purchases of new issues at the post office to exactly what you need for your collection. Avoid buying duplicates for investment; new issues usually do not rise in value enough to offset the cost of holding them. And if you want to get the most for your money, collect singles, not multiples such as blocks and panes.

As mentioned earlier, the market offers a tremendous variety of U.S. albums, ranging from solid, no-frills basics to magnificent, top-of-the-line hingeless albums. Check with your local dealer or with a mail order supply firm.

PLATE BLOCKS

Plate block collecting has been popular for decades. A plate block consists of four or more stamps on whose selvage appears a printing plate number or numbers. Every printing plate used to print U.S. stamps is assigned a plate number for security purposes. Plates are logged on press and a record kept of every impression made from each plate. Thousands of sheets are printed from each plate and each of these bears the same plate number. Printing a large or extended issue requires dozens and sometimes even hundreds of plates, each of which has its own plate number.

Plate block of 6 at left; plate block of 4 at right.

From the 1920s to the late 1960s, most plate blocks consisted of either four or six stamps, depending on the placement of the plate number in the selvage. Rotary press issues of the period usually contained plate numbers in the corner selvage; flat plate issues, toward the center of the selvage. Plate numbers appearing in the corner of a pane are collected in blocks of four. Plate numbers appearing elsewhere on the selvage are collected in blocks of six (or more depending on the number of plate numbers) with the plate number(s) usually positioned on the center selvage tab (or tabs) for aesthetic balance. It is crucial that the plate number appear on the center selvage tab(s) of these issues rather than to the left or right of center. If the plate number(s) do not appear on the center tab(s), the block is not a plate block and not worth the premium a plate block commands, which can be as much as ten times or more the value of the stamps as individual items.

With the arrival of multicolor printing in the late 1960s, the postal service began spreading numbers (one for each of the four or more plates used in the color printing process) up and down the

selvage, as illustrated at left. Plate blocks grew as large as eight, ten, even twelve stamps or more. Lately, however, the postal service has condensed the placement of plate numbers to one or two corner selvage tabs. Now nearly all plate blocks consist of four stamps; however, exceptions exist. Specialized U.S. catalogues list the precise number of stamps necessary to constitute a plate block for each issue.

Most plate block collectors try to acquire a plate block of each issue. However, plate blocks simply do not exist for many nineteenth-century stamps, so absolute completion is impossible. Those nineteenth-century plate blocks that do exist are scarce and expensive, usually beginning in the low thousands and running as high as $150,000 or more. As a practical matter, most plate block collectors begin with current issues and work their way back as far as their budget allows.

Some collectors try to obtain an example of every plate number used to print a certain issue. Even more ambitious collectors attempt to put together a collection of every plate number and every position for their favorite issue. Between the mid-1930s and the 1980s, most stamps were printed in press sheets containing four panes with plate numbers located in the corners of each pane: upper right pane with plate number in the upper right corner, and so forth. A set of plate numbers, one for each position on a press sheet, is known as a matched set. Collecting matched sets can be quite challenging, especially for definitives in use over an extended period of time. For example, more than 350 plates (resulting in more than 1,400 different positions and numbers) were used to print the 3-cent Presidential definitive in use between 1938 and 1954.

Nowadays, press sheets contain six or more panes per sheet, and the Postal Service often prints plate numbers in each of the four corners of the panes (especially on compact sheets), so the position of the plate number is no longer a reliable indicator of a pane's position on a press sheet. Instead, the position of a pane is shown by a diagram appearing in the selvage.

The *Durland Standard Plate Number Catalog*, published by the Bureau Issues Association, contains a comprehensive listing of U.S. plate numbers and positions.

PLATE NUMBER COILS

Since 1981, plate numbers have also appeared on coil stamps, giving rise to one of the most popular specialties in U.S. philately—plate number coil (PNC) collecting. Before 1981, coil plate numbers were trimmed off in the finishing process as the stamps were slit apart and rolled into coils.

Next time you buy a roll of stamps, unwind it slowly, keeping an eye toward the bottom of the stamps. Soon you'll encounter a stamp with a tiny plate number (or numbers, in the case of multi-colored stamps) underneath the design. You will have found a PNC. Plate numbers appear at various intervals (such as every 25

**Contemporary cover with PNC single. Note the plate number
at the bottom of the stamp.**

or 52 stamps) depending on the type of printing plate used, so
PNCs of some issues are more abundant than others. PNCs are
collected in strips, usually of three or five stamps, with the plate
number positioned on the center stamp. The number *must* be on
the center stamp or it is not considered a collectible strip. Some
collectors try to acquire every number used to print a given issue,
which is typically anywhere from one or two plates up to a
maximum of perhaps twenty-five.

PNC collectors look for covers bearing stamps with plate
numbers, especially scarce numbers. Columns in philatelic
periodicals keep collectors up-to-date on scarce numbers. Every
household and business in America receive a steady supply of bulk
mail containing coil stamps. Keep your eyes open for covers with
PNCs.

PNC collecting is popular because it's relatively new,
sufficiently challenging to make it interesting, yet not so complex
or expensive that completion is impossible. The essential reference
for PNC collectors is *Linn's Plate Number Coil Handbook* by Ken
Lawrence.

FIRST DAY COVERS

First day covers (FDCs) contain stamps cancelled on the first
day they were available for public sale. Until the twentieth
century, the postal service seldom announced an official first day
of sale for new stamps. They just shipped stamps to post offices,

which placed them on sale as they saw fit. Today, however, the USPS announces an official first day of issue for each new stamp. Usually (but not always) a new stamp is placed on sale in only a single city (known as the official city) on its first day of issue. The stamp goes on sale nationwide the following day. Most first day covers are postmarked in the official city with a special cancel containing the words "First Day of Issue."

You can send in your own covers for first day cancellation; however, most FDC collectors subscribe to a new-issue service to avoid the inconvenience of preparing and mailing their own covers and to ensure that they don't miss an issue. Ordering from a service also eliminates the risk of having a cover damaged or over-cancelled on its journey through the mailstream.

Some collectors specialize. They try to obtain an example of every cachet produced by a particular cachet maker. Others collectors concentrate on a specific stamp, such as the statehood stamp of their home state, and try to collect every different cachet produced for it—and there can be dozens and dozens.

Hand-painted first day cover.

Still others prefer hand-colored or hand-painted cachets, which are usually done in very limited quantities (typically 10 to 75), and tend to hold their value more than mass-produced cachets. Cachet artists use watercolor, acrylic, colored pencil, and occasionally other media to execute their designs. The results are vivid and spectacular, usually much more eye-arresting than mass-produced covers. Some collect just the covers of their favorite artist or artists; others try to acquire as many covers of their favorite stamp painted by as many artists as possible.

Purists eschew add-ons (cachets painted on older FDCs years after the cover was issued) and insist on covers painted contemporaneously with the issuance of the stamp. Another school collects add-ons avidly; it's mostly a matter of preference. Prices for hand-painted covers by recognized FDC artists, such as Dorothy Knapp (a pioneer in the hand-painted cachet field), can run into hundreds of dollars. Hand-painted new issues are generally priced from $10 to $75.

Hand-colored cachets differ from hand-painted cachets in that the outline of a design is first printed on a cover, then areas within the design are colored by hand. Hand-colored cachets are usually issued in larger editions—sometimes as many as several hundred—and typically sell for less than hand-painted cachets.

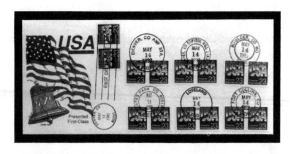

FDC bearing both official and unofficial cancels.

The postal service allows a grace period (usually 30 days) from the date of issue, during which time one can obtain a first day cancellation. This means that not all FDCs are actually cancelled on their first day of issue, a fact that doesn't bother most collectors. However, purists insist on *actual* first day cancellations. To get them, they buy newly issued stamps at the first day city, prepare covers, then drive to post offices in other towns and cities to have them cancelled, usually by hand. Since the grace period applies only to the official city, covers bearing postmarks from any other place dated on the first day of issue must, by necessity, have been cancelled on that day only, and are first day covers in the truest sense of the word. Such FDCs are known as unofficial first day covers. Ironically, "unofficial" covers are indisputably more authentic than "official" covers.

FDC collectors prefer cacheted covers; however, few cachet makers operated prior to 1935, so cacheted covers prior to that date are the exception rather than the rule and worth a premium. Collectors generally insist that FDCs produced after 1935 have cachets. FDCs produced after 1935 without cachets generally have little value, unless the stamp on the cover itself is valuable.

Collectors also prefer unaddressed FDCs (covers that have not been addressed) where possible. Unaddressed FDCs are seldom available for issues produced before 1945. This because in those days, FDCs were returned to cachet makers as individual pieces of mail in the regular mailstream. Later, cachet makers were able to have covers returned in bulk, eliminating the necessity of having to individually address them. Unaddressed FDCs produced before 1945 sell for a premium because of their scarcity. Most FDCs produced after 1945 are unaddressed and carry no premium; instead, addressed covers of the period sell for a discount.

Dealers often stock starter assortments of 100 or more post-1945 FDCs at very reasonable prices.

The *Scott U.S. First Day Cover Catalogue* is an excellent general catalogue that lists and prices all FDCs, including premiums applicable to cachets of the major cachet producers. The *Planty Photo Encyclopedia of Cacheted First Day Covers* zeroes in on the classic period, 1901 through 1939. It illustrates and prices every known cachet from the period, many of which are quite valuable. It's a must for the serious collector.

Before the year 1920, the postal service made no special effort to announce issue dates for definitive stamps, and few commemoratives existed. Even after it began announcing dates of issue, most collectors remained uninterested in obtaining FDCs. Consequently, few first day covers made prior to 1920 exist. Those that do are generally worth hundreds or even thousands of dollars. Early first day covers do not bear the slogan cancel "First Day of Issue," and they lack cachets. The date on the postmark is the only clue. Treasures disguised as ordinary looking covers wait to be discovered, if you know what to look for, and are willing to take the time to check.

First day covers for stamps issued before 1900 are rare. So collectors go after EKU (earliest known use) covers, i.e., covers postmarked as near to the first day of issue as possible. Sometimes the earliest known use is only a few days after actual issue date of the stamp; other times it's weeks or months later. Nineteenth-century EKU covers are rare; often no more than a single example per issue exists. Prices generally start in the low thousands and run as high as $125,000.

Today, stamps are occasionally sold and used before their official first day of issue, giving rise to the modern early use cover. Early use of modern stamps occurs because post offices receive supplies of stamps well in advance of their issue date. With so many new stamps constantly arriving, clerks cannot always keep track of which is supposed to be issued when, especially during hectic periods such as Christmas. Most modern early use covers are discovered by collectors checking dates on incoming mail. The most fertile ground for discovering early use covers is in correspondence received by large-volume mail recipients such as utility companies and insurance companies. Although not worth a lot of money, modern early use covers are avidly collected by specialists. Information about forthcoming and recently issued stamps appears in all philatelic newspapers.

Membership in the American First Day Cover Society (AFDCS) is recommended for anyone seriously interested in first day covers. The AFDCS publishes a thick journal eight times a year. It's loaded with articles devoted to FDC collecting.

SINGLE STAMP OR SERIES

Some collectors are fascinated by a single series, such the 1869 pictorials, the Washington-Franklin series, or the Liberty series, and limit their collections to stamps of the series. Others narrow their focus even further, concentrating on a single stamp. They study the stamp in infinite detail, collect all varieties including plate flaws, color shades, and paper and gum varieties.

Specializing in a single stamp or single series is nothing new. In the early years, before commemoratives existed, serious philatelists collected, studied, and documented the definitive stamps of their era, stamps that today are classics. It is beyond the financial resources of most collectors to build a collection of one of the nineteenth-century classic issues, but one can still derive the same sense of challenge and discovery by specializing in a modern issue, such as a definitive stamp or series, especially one rife with varieties. Many of the stamps we take for granted will be of interest to future generations of collectors, just as stamps issued years ago continue to fascinate us today. A small but growing number of collectors are beginning to study modern definitives because the raw material is readily available and can often be had for the asking. The quest is usually more time-intensive than cash-intensive.

Students of single-stamp and single-series studies immerse themselves in an issue. They find the challenge of discovery more satisfying than the routine of buying new issues. They search out and assemble collections of shades, printing and perforation varieties, gum varieties, examples on cover illustrating rates and usages, and even counterfeits.

Examples of the 1954 Liberty Series.

The Liberty series of 1954 is a good example. Although at first glance it appears very straightforward (27 sheet stamps, 8 coil stamps, 2 booklet panes), specialists have discovered a myriad of collectible varieties: wet printings and dry printings; large hole coils and small hole coils; tagged and untagged varieties—some of which are elusive and valuable. There even exist two values counterfeited by the North Koreans to mail propaganda to South Korea. Liberty series specialists have discovered these varieties through research and study, often acquiring examples for next to nothing because the Liberty series is so recent no one pays much attention to it. But, the great rarities of the Liberty series are just as elusive as many of the classic rarities. It would be hard to put a price on any of the best Liberty specialized collections because none has come to market, but the best among them would easily fetch thousands of dollars.

Increasingly, collectors are discovering that single-stamp and single-series specialization yield great dividends, both in terms of enjoyment and profit.

OTHER SPECIALTIES

State Postmarks. Some collectors try to obtain a postmark from every post office in their state. The challenge arises in finding covers from DPOs (discontinued post offices), especially the boom-and-bust ghost towns of the West, many of which operated for only a short time, sometimes less than year. Collectors of state postmarks inevitably become immersed in the history of their state, increasing their knowledge and understanding of the area in which they live. Most collectors insist on complete covers. Postmarks cut from the covers, no matter how neatly, are worth little. Books on state post offices exist for many states.

Precancels. Precancels bearing city and state overprints are collected in much the same fashion as postmarks of states, except that precancels are almost always collected off cover and mounted on album pages. Precancel collecting is generally less expensive than state-postmark cover collecting. Most examples can be obtained for less than half a dollar. Precancel collectors often collect by state. Town collectors try to obtain one precancel from each town that issued them; town and type collectors try to obtain one precancel of each type from each town (towns often made use of several different precancelling devices over the course of years, which are known as types). Bureau precancel collectors attempt to get a copy of every precancel printed by the Bureau of Engraving and Printing. Contact the Precancel Stamp Society for more information on this fascinating specialty.

State duck stamp at left; federal duck stamp at right.

Duck Stamps. Philatelists, hunters, and conservationists alike enjoy collecting the large, colorful waterfowl hunting stamps issued by the Department of Interior (known as federal duck stamps). The first was issued in 1934. Most stamp catalogues list duck stamps. States began issuing duck stamps in the early 1970s. Few people collect issues of all states; most prefer to concentrate on those of their state.

An EFO with paper fold at left; with color shift at right.

Errors and EFOs. More and more collectors are becoming intrigued with major errors and EFOs (errors, freaks, and oddities; generally, minor kinds of errors). Major errors tend to be more expensive than other kinds of stamps because they exist in small quantities; however, there are fewer to collect and they hold their value well. EFOs are both fascinating and inexpensive. Some collectors concentrate on an issue or topic, such as space, while others concentrate on finding a certain type of error, such as misperforated stamps, foldovers, or color shifts. The Errors, Freaks and Oddities Collector's Club (EFOCC) publishes an informative newsletter, which contains an auction loaded with every kind of odd-looking stamp you could imagine.

Special delivery stamp (left); parcel post stamp (right).

Back of the Book (B-O-B). Back of the book collecting appeals to those who prefer smaller, generally finite issues such as airmails, special deliveries, and postage dues, all of which the United States no longer issues. B-O-B includes revenues and other issues that appear after listings for definitives and commemoratives in catalogues, hence the name back of the book.

These are just a few examples of what U.S. collecting has to offer. The opportunities are limited only by your imagination.

CONDITION & GRADING

Realtors are fond of saying that the three primary elements of property value are location, location, and location. In philately, rarity notwithstanding, the three main elements of value are condition, condition, and condition. The same stamp that sells for $500 in superb, never-hinged condition can often be bought for $50 in faulty condition. It is fair to say that 90 percent of the value of the superb stamp represents a premium for condition.

If you're just beginning and working with inexpensive stamps, don't be overly concerned about condition—this because inexpensive stamps don't vary much in price from one to another. As you begin to acquire more expensive stamps, condition becomes an issue because it affects price so dramatically. Be aware of condition, but don't become obsessed by it.

Condition is the sum of a stamp's elements: gum, hinging, centering, margins, color, freshness, perforations, cancellations, and faults.

CAUTION: Old stamps are fragile. Don't tamper with them or try to improve their appearance; it is risky. You're likely to do more harm than good, even if you think you're being careful. Don't remove stamps from envelopes or postcards; the intact item may be worth more, by virtue of its postmark or other markings, than the stamps by themselves. And for the same reason, don't cut the corners off old envelopes. Don't attempt to separate stamps that are stuck together or stuck down to album pages; you may cause damage and reduce their value. Don't attempt to clean stamps; you'll only reduce their value. Leave everything intact. Rely on an experienced person such as a stamp dealer to give you advice on how to proceed.

GUM

Gum is the single most important element of condition of a mint stamp.

Original gum (OG)—gum applied at the time of manufacture. Until late in the twentieth century, usually composed of gum arabic or dextrine, which are smooth and glossy in appearance. Some recent gums (such as polyvinyl alcohol gums) have a dull, matte-like appearance. Original gum is prized. Stamps with full original gum are worth considerably more than stamps with partial gum or no gum.

Tropical gum—gum that has been affected by high humidity, often losing its gloss, and often discolored, either uniformly or in spots caused by microorganisms.

Glazed gum—gum partially liquified then resolidified, often the result of humidity, poor storage, or poor mounting. The degree to which value is affected depends on the degree of glazing, the rarity of the issue, and the normal condition of gum on the issue.

Disturbed gum (DG)—often arising from an attempt to remove a stamp hinge by the application of moisture, a process that leaves gum in a mess and can even warp the stamp.

No gum (NG)—lacking gum. The term "no gum" implies that a stamp originally possessed gum, which was later removed, hence an inferior state of condition. Stamps issued without gum are referred to as "without gum" or "ungummed" rather than "no gum" to make the distinction that they are "as issued" and not impaired.

Regummed (RG)—regumming is a process intended to improve the appearance and salability of a stamp by applying new gum to simulate original gum. Regumming need not be contemporary; it may have been done years before. In philately, unlike other fields where restoration is encouraged, any attempt to improve the appearance of a stamp by adding new gum, new perforations, or alter it in any way from its original state, is frowned upon. Regummed stamps are regarded as damaged goods and held in such low esteem, that they trade at enormous discounts, typically only 10 to 20 percent of catalogue value. The premium for original gum on stamps has led to the practice of regumming.

HINGING

Until the middle of the twentieth century, collectors used hinges to mount stamps, which is why so few early stamps survive without hinge marks. Today, collectors of mint stamps generally favor plastic stamp mounts because mounts do not affect gum. The better the state of a stamp's original gum, the greater its value.

Early stamp hinges were often just bits of ordinary paper attached with whatever glue was handy, usually utilitarian glues made to hold things together. As a consequence, old-time hinges are difficult to remove. At best, they disturb a stamp's gum when removed. At worst, they take part of the stamp's paper with them, leaving a thin spot (known as a thin). Early commercially produced hinges were little better. More often than not, they leave gum horrendously disturbed when removed.

Frequently, the only way to remove such a hinge is to soak it off. Hinges are sometimes soaked off heavily hinged stamps, especially early ones, to improve their appearance. The absence of gum on the back of such a stamp is often more appealing than gum discolored and disturbed by the presence of an ugly hinge remnant. That's why so few early stamps survive with original gum.

Glassine hinges coated with light adhesives appeared later, advertised as being peelable. Peelable hinges generally cause no damage when carefully removed; nevertheless, they still leave a hinge mark, albeit light. Today, collectors tend to insist on the best, most pristine examples of mint stamps possible, and that means never-hinged stamps. Although lightly hinged stamps are not considered faulty, they are generally less desirable than never-hinged examples. Never-hinged stamps command a premium; hinged stamps sell at a discount; no-gum and regummed stamps sell at a substantial discount.

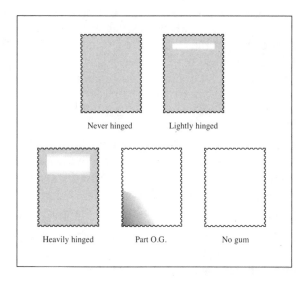

Never hinged   Lightly hinged

Heavily hinged   Part O.G.   No gum

CAUTION: Don't attempt to remove hinges that resist peeling unless you have experience. You're likely to cause damage and diminish the value of your stamps. If a hinge won't peel off with a gentle tug, leave it alone. You're better off with a heavily hinged stamp than a thinned stamp. And, always use stamp tongs to handle stamps. Even the faint, colorless imprint left on gum by a finger on a humid day will reduce a stamp's value, especially an expensive one.

The descriptions of gum and hinging below are followed by standard abbreviations where applicable.

Never hinged (NH)—a stamp that has never had a stamp hinge applied. Original gum is implied. A regummed stamp is never referred to as never hinged.

Lightly hinged (LH)—a stamp whose hinge mark is barely noticeable.

Heavily hinged (HH)—a stamp whose hinge (or part of it) is still in place, being so firmly attached that it is impossible to remove without damaging the stamp, or a stamp whose hinge has been removed leaving a distinct and unappealing mark on its gum.

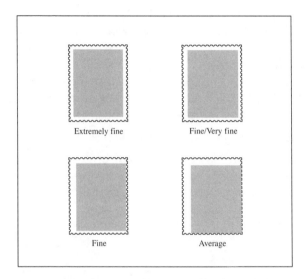

Extremely fine   Fine/Very fine

Fine   Average

The following symbols are often used in advertising and auction catalogues to indicate the state of gum: ★★ never hinged; ★ hinged; (★) without original gum, unused.

Part original gum (part OG)—possessing only part original gum, the missing portion presumably lost during the removal of a hinge or when moisture was applied to loosen a stamp that had been attached to an album page by its own gum.

Disturbed gum (DG)—refer to the description in the previous section on gum.

CENTERING

What the condition of gum is to the back of a stamp, centering is to the front. Centering refers to the way in which a stamp's design is situated in relation to its margins. The more balanced the margins, the more visually appealing the stamp. Stamps with balanced margins are referred to as well-centered. Stamps whose margins are not reasonably balanced are referred to as off-center or poorly centered. Collectors prefer perforations to be clear of a stamp's design and the design to be as evenly balanced within the margins as possible.

Nineteenth-century stamps—both U.S. and foreign—are notoriously poorly centered. In many cases, designers left almost no room between stamps, which resulted in perforations touching or cutting into a design on at least one side. Modern stamps tend to be well centered, so finding nicely centered copies is usually not difficult. The characteristics of each issue must be taken into account when determining the grade of centering.

Standard grades of centering include:

Extremely fine (EF or XF)—well centered, margins almost perfectly balanced.

Very fine (VF)—moderately centered.

Fine (F)—poorly centered, yet perforations clear of the design.

Average (Avg.)—very poorly centered, perforations touching or cutting into the design—a real dog.

A variety of split grades, such as F-VF (fine to very fine), describe finer shadings. The term "superb" is occasionally applied to a stamp that is perfectly centered, as well as being pristine in all other respects. Catalogues typically list prices for only a single grade, usually in the middle of the spectrum, often F-VF, but sometimes VF. Therefore, the actual price of an individual stamp may be higher or lower than catalogue value, depending on its exact grade.

OTHER ELEMENTS

Color—how vivid or pronounced color is within the range of shades known to exist for a given stamp. The older the stamp, the more important freshness and intensity of color becomes. Old stamps tend to become drab with age. Papers tend to yellow; ink pigments tend to fade. Color is judged on how near it is to the issued state. A stamp's color must be measured against others of its kind, not against issues that are routinely boldly colored. Adjectives such as "vivid," "bold," "bright," and "intense" are used to describe stamps with premium color. Degradation of color is usually a problem associated with age and not so much an issue on newer stamps.

Freshness—how near to original post office state a stamp is. Ideally, a stamp possesses "mint bloom" and pristine paper. Again, the older the stamp, the more difficult it is to find in a state of pristine freshness. Knowledgeable collectors avoid "toned" stamps, i.e., stamps turned yellowish or brownish, often from storage in albums or stock books made of cheap paper.

The stamp at left has normal margins for issue; the stamp at right has jumbo margins.

Margins—the size of a stamp's margins, as distinct from centering. Individual stamps possessing margins larger than normal for their issue are highly prized by collectors. The larger than normal (for issue) the margins, the more desirable the stamp. Oversized margins are referred to as jumbo or boardwalk margins. Some issues normally possess large margins, so each stamp must be judged according to what is normal for its issue.

Cancel (cancellation)—the ideal cancel is neat, clear and neither distracts from nor obliterates the underlying design of the stamp. It is legitimate and contemporaneous to the stamp. Collectors avoid favor cancels and contrived cancels, especially on expensive stamps. Expensive stamps whose mint and used prices are the same or nearly the same are often encountered with bogus cancels because clean used copies are more salable than no-gum or heavily hinged mint copies. Hence the emphasis on the words "legitimate" and "contemporaneous." Colored and specialty cancels can be worth a considerable premium on early United States stamps. Check a specialized catalogue for more specific information. Pen cancels on early issues sell at a discount. Pen cancels

Light cancels (left) are preferred; heavy cancels (right) are avoided.

on modern stamps are considered faults, and the stamps are usually unsalable at any price. Revenue cancels and CTOs are generally worth considerably less than postal cancels.

Perforations—the ideal is to have perforation teeth (perfs) as uniform as possible within the limits of the issue. Most early stamps have irregular perforations, which is not considered a fault. Sometimes one or more perf teeth are shorter than others on a row or are missing entirely. They are referred to as short perfs or pulled perfs. Issues with large or widely spaced perforation holes are prone to separate irregularly and for them, irregular perfs are considered the norm. Copies of such stamps possessing perfect rows of teeth sell for a premium. The condition of perfs must be viewed within the context of what is usual for an issue.

The stamp at left contains a pulled perf at bottom and irregular perfs on its upper right side; the stamp at right is normal for issue.

Don't be too nit-picky about perforations. Most modern issues routinely come with uniform, balanced perforations, and collectors really don't pay much attention to their condition unless it is visually distracting.   Nor do they pay much attention to the condition of perfs on inexpensive stamps.   The condition of perfs becomes more important on early stamps and expensive stamps.

Reperforating is a process of adding perforations to improve the appearance of a straight-edged stamp or to improve centering by trimming a margin and adding perforations.   Reperforated stamps are worth only a small fraction of catalogue value.

Faults—tears, thins, pinholes, creases, surface scuffs, abrasions, stains, foxing, discoloration, glazed or tropicalized gum—anything

**These stamps catalogue nearly $300;
however, with pieces missing, they are worthless.**

that might be construed as damage—are considered major faults. Minor or trivial faults include such things as bent perforations or perforation thins.   The vast majority of nineteenth-century stamps are faulty.   The earlier the stamp, the greater the likelihood it will be faulty.   Stamps without faults are referred to as sound.   Grades of condition that might otherwise apply to a sound stamp, do not apply to a faulty stamp; faulty stamps go directly to the lowest price bracket.   Stamps with pieces missing are virtually worthless.

Thins are usually the result of careless hinge removal and are visible from the back.   Again, do not attempt to remove hinges from valuable stamps without the help of an experienced person. Creases may be visible to the naked eye or visible only in watermark fluid; either way, they're considered faults.   Sometimes stamps with faults are "improved."   Creases are ironed out, discolorations bleached, pinholes and thins filled, scuffs and abrasions carefully colored to match original ink. Stamps that have been repaired or improved are considered faulty nonetheless. Faulty stamps and improved stamps are worth only a small fraction of catalogue value, typically five to fifteen percent. The precise amount depends on the degree of the fault. The only exception is in the case of extremely rare stamps that do not exist in sound condition.

In many cases, faults and improvements are not obvious. It is prudent to check stamps carefully for any sign of tampering, especially when spending a significant amount for a stamp. (More about improvements in the chapter "Fakes and Forgeries.")

Natural inclusions (material embedded in paper during its manufacture), irregular perforations that are normal for an issue, and natural gum skips and gum bends (unless severe enough to have broken the paper fibers of the underlying stamp), while not technically faults, are elements avoided by the most demanding buyers. The absence of these elements generally increases the value of a stamp. Again, collectors of inexpensive stamps generally don't pay much attention things such as natural inclusions and gum skips.

Elements, such as straight edges (collectors prefer stamps with perforations on all four sides, except in the case of coil stamps, booklet stamps, and imperforates), heavy cancels, and exceedingly poor centering, while technically not faults, nevertheless, reduce the value of a stamp to a small fraction of catalogue value.

In summary, condition is everything. Individual stamps are priced according to their merits; the higher the grade, the more costly the stamp. You need not be overly concerned about condition in the beginning, especially when working with common, inexpensive stamps. Later, as your degree of sophistication grows and you begin to acquire more expensive stamps, you'll need to be aware of the fine points of condition.

CONSERVATION

Stamps, especially old ones, are fragile objects that must be handled and stored with care. The three great enemies of stamps are light, heat, and moisture. Avoid these hazards as much as possible.

Don't display stamps in direct light for prolonged periods. Pigments are prone to fading, paper to yellowing. Sunlight is especially bad; fluorescent light, not much better. Even the use of UV glass to screen out ultraviolet light will not protect against other wavelengths, which can also cause damage over time, although more subtly. Short-term exposure to light, such as exhibiting at a show, is not a danger.

More stamps are ruined by moisture than by any other hazard. Moisture in all forms (water, humidity, dampness) is deadly. Keep stamps as dry as possible. Always store stamp albums upright so they can breathe. Never store albums flat, especially piled one atop another, because the weight causes stamps to stick, especially under humid conditions. Even stamps in glassines are susceptible to moisture and pressure. Once they become stuck together, only soaking will separate them, and their gum will be lost. Album paper absorbs humidity like a sponge, but loses it only slowly. A few humid days can expose stamps to weeks of dampness. Albums should be opened and allowed to dry any time they have been exposed to abnormal humidity. Humidity wreaks such havoc on gum that some collectors in places such as Hawaii and the Caribbean collect only used stamps.

Moisture also promotes the growth of mold and mildew, which discolor stamps and attack gum. Even stamps without gum are susceptible to mildew and foxing (discoloration by microorganisms). Avoid storing stamps in places prone to dampness or leaks, such as basements, storage sheds, and barns. Don't store stamps near water pipes. Even safe-deposit boxes are not one hundred percent safe. In some cases, stamps in fireproof bank vaults have been ruined by sprinklers set off by a fire in another part of the bank (we have no idea what sprinklers were doing inside a *fireproof* vault). In some cases, safe-deposit vaults located below ground level have been flooded by broken water mains or springtime downpours, perils that do not affect vaults located above ground. Subterranean vaults are also more prone to dampness from ground water.

Keep stamps away from heat, which compounds the effects of moisture. Avoid storing stamp albums on shelves exposed to direct sunlight. Avoid attics and garages, which are likewise prone to overheating. Exposure to heat and moisture causes stamps to curl, often so badly that attempting to uncurl them ruins them. Dry heat is no better. It causes stamps to become brittle and gum to crack. In severe cases, cracked gum cracks a stamp's paper, thus ruining it. Prolonged exposure to dramatic temperature swings causes expansion and contraction, weakening a stamp's paper fibers, just as bending a piece of wire repeatedly weakens it.

Keep stamps away from dust and dirt. Windblown grit, the kind that accumulates in garages and sheds, acts like sandpaper, if ever so subtly. Keep stamps away from insects. Even seemingly innocuous ones can be dangerous. Crickets love the flavor of some gums and eagerly nibble away portions of stamps possessing it.

A few more don'ts. Never use any kind of tape to mount stamps or covers. Keep tape—adhesive, cellophane, whatever the kind—away from your collection. Don't use it on stamps, on album pages, on glassines, or to secure the sides of mounts. Don't use tape on anything stamp-related—period.

Don't mount or store newspaper clippings next to stamps. Newspaper yellows and degrades with the passing of time. The chemicals that cause yellowing migrate into any other paper they come in contact with—stamps, covers, album pages. Discard old glassines or anything else that has yellowed with age. The jury's still out on recycled paper, which is treated with chemicals to bleach and whiten it. In general, avoid papers with a strong chemical odor. It may take years to know what effects, if any, recycling chemicals have on paper. Meanwhile, avoid the risk of exposing your stamps to it.

Keep rubber bands away from stamps. They contain a sulphur compound that discolors some pigments. And there's nothing worse than a rubber band that's dried out or melted, and adhered to whatever it's come in contact with.

Don't use paper clips on stamps or anywhere that might leave a mark on a stamp. Some paper clips rust, especially in humid climates, leaving spots on anything they've come in contact with.

And remember, avoid storing stamps in anything made of softened plastic such as vinyl. The softer the plastic, the more softening agent (visible as an oily iridescent film or smelling strongly of new-car smell). The softening agent, which is petro-chemical based, has been known to discolor stamps and in some cases, leach the color out of some printing inks and absorb it into the plastic. Unsoftened (free of softening agent) vinyl is fairly inert, as are Mylar and polypropolene. And don't store stamps in variety-store photo albums, especially the kind with waxed or self-adhesive pages, even those advertised as low-tack.

Don't remove stamps from covers or postcards; usually they have more value than the stamps by themselves. Don't attempt to separate stamps that are stuck together or stuck down to album pages; you'll only cause damage and reduce their value. Don't attempt to clean stamps; you'll do more harm than good.

A few do's.

Fingers contain moisture, oil, and often small amounts of grime. Make sure your hands are clean before working with stamps and always use stamp tongs to handle stamps.

Use materials made specifically for the hobby. If it wasn't made for stamps, think twice about using it.

Insure stamps if they have any significant value. Most homeowner's policies cover collectibles, but their limits of liability are low, typically $300 or so, without a special rider. The APS offers an excellent, low-cost policy that covers most risks, such as fire and theft. Their policy's limits of liability are higher and premiums lower than those of most standard casualty policies. Check the Resource Guide under insurance providers. In many cases, insurance is less expensive than paying safe-deposit rent, especially for bulky collections. Before spending hundreds of dollars a year on safe-deposit storage, compare the cost with insurance. Also, be aware that unless the contents of a safe-deposit box are insured, they're at risk from loss by fire, theft, and natural disaster. Almost all banks refuse to accept liability for the contents of a safe-deposit box for any reason. Check your box rental agreement.

In summary, use common sense in handling and storing stamps. Keep them away from light, heat, moisture, and dirt. Avoid storing stamps in basements, garages, storage sheds, and attics. To the degree possible, store stamps in an area with constant temperature and humidity. Use high quality materials, those intended specifically for use with stamps. Insure stamps if they have significant value.

Rare stamps

The British Guiana one-cent magenta and the U.S. inverted Jenny (the stamp with the upside down airplane) are two of the most famous and most valuable stamps in the world. A school boy discovered one; a clerk discovered the other on his way to work.

The World's Rarest Stamp
The British Guiana one-cent magenta is often referred to as the world's rarest stamp or the world's most valuable stamp. Although only a single copy is known to exist, the one-cent magenta cannot accurately be described as the world's rarest stamp because a number of other stamps exist for which only a single copy is known. It is arguably the world's most expensive stamp because no single stamp off cover has ever sold for as much, $935,000 in 1980. The unique Alexandria, Virginia, postmaster's provisional issued in 1846, known as the Blue Boy by virtue of being printed on blue paper, reportedly sold by private treaty for $1 million in 1981. However, the Blue Boy was on cover and rare stamps on cover are generally regarded as more valuable than those off cover. It is argued that had the Blue Boy not been on cover, it would have sold for less. So in the minds of most, the one-cent magenta is still the world's single most valuable stamp. And there is no question that the British Guiana one-cent magenta is the world's best-known rarity.

The one-cent magenta, so called because it is printed on a deep wine-red paper, is not a particularly attractive stamp but a crude

The British Guiana one-cent magenta.

attempt by a local printer to make something that would pass for a postage stamp. In 1856, when the one-cent magenta was printed, British Guiana was a remote outpost of the British Empire located north of Brazil in South America, and its printing facilities were rudimentary. The stamp's central feature is a stock printer's cut of a ship around which appear the name of the colony, the value of the stamp, and a Latin motto. Somewhere along the line, someone trimmed the corners off the stamp, giving it its trademark octagonal shape. Most would say the stamp is ugly. Perhaps young L. Vernon Vaughan, the boy who discovered it in 1863, thought so too, which may have been the reason he decided to part with it for 6 shillings (about $1.50), or perhaps he thought a better copy might come along.

He sold it to a man named N.R. McKinnon, who added it to his stamp collection. McKinnon kept it for several years, then sold it to Thomas Ridpath, a stamp dealer from Liverpool, England. Ridpath sold it to Count Ferrari, who at the time was the world's most avid stamp collector. (More about Ferrari in "Famous Collectors.") Ferrari appreciated the one-cent magenta's rarity and did not quibble over the $700 or so it cost him—the exact figure is not clear. He kept the stamp until his death in 1917.

By the time Ferrari's vast collection came to market in the 1920s, knowledgeable collectors throughout the world had begun to appreciate the true rarity of the one-cent magenta. It was the one stamp necessary to complete King George V of Great Britain's collection of the British Empire. In addition to George V, Maurice Burrus, the Swiss tobacco magnate, and Arthur Hind, the wealthy American textile manufacturer, wanted the stamp and competed for it when Ferrari's collection appeared at auction. When the dust settled, Hind had outbid his rivals, securing the one-cent magenta for the then-record price of $32,500.

Hind kept the stamp until he died in 1933, at which time it passed to his widow. She held it until 1940, then sold it by private treaty to a collector named Frederick T. Small for about $40,000. Small owned the stamp until 1970, when he offered it through Robert A. Siegel's Rarities of the World auction, where it sold for a record price of $280,000. The new owners, a syndicate of investors headed by Pennsylvania stamp dealer Irwin Weinberg, held the stamp until 1980, when it again appeared in Robert A. Siegel's annual Rarities of the World sale. Many felt the one-cent magenta would surpass the $1 million mark, especially in a boom stamp market then fueled by inflation. It came close. The bidding stopped at $850,000 ($935,000 including the 10 percent buyer's premium), just shy of $1 million. The anonymous buyer was later revealed to be John E. duPont.

From time to time, one hears rumors of a second example of the one-cent magenta, but as of this writing, none has been confirmed.

The Inverted Jenny

On the morning of May 14, 1918, William T. Robey, a cashier at Hibbs and Company in Washington, D.C., stopped on his way to work to purchase some of the new bi-colored 24-cent airmail stamps that were being placed on sale that day. The stamp featured a Curtiss Jenny biplane printed in blue surrounded by a carmine frame. Robey, an enthusiastic stamp collector, planned to use some of the new stamps on first flight covers that were to be carried by airplane to Philadelphia and New York the next day. He asked the clerk for a pane of one hundred, which the clerk pulled from his drawer and laid on the counter. When Robey saw that the airplane was upside down, his heart stood still. He quickly tendered payment, hoping the clerk would not notice the error, tucked the pane away and hurried off to work. At work, he showed the odd-looking stamps to fellow employees, and during the course of the day, shared the news of his find via telephone with friends. The word spread like wildfire. Soon eager collectors hurried to post offices all over the city hoping to discover more inverts.

The inverted Jenny.

Having been alerted by the inadvertent remarks of error seekers, postal inspectors visited Robey at his office that afternoon, demanding to see the error pane. When Robey refused, they threatened to confiscate it. Robey stood his ground, and the postal inspectors finally left in a huff. After work, Robey visited the office of a Washington stamp dealer named Hamilton F. Colman, where a group of collectors had gathered to see Robey's error pane. Earlier in the day, Colman had offered Robey $500 for it, but Robey declined. Robey asked the group what they thought the pane ought to be worth, but no one had a firm opinion. One fellow reminded Robey that stamps were printed in press sheets of 400, then cut into panes of 100 for sale over the counter, so it was possible that more panes might exist. The more that existed, the less Robey's pane would be worth. However, unbeknownst to Robey and his friends, the 24-cent airmail had been printed one pane of 100 at a time. Nor did they know that as soon as the government learned of the error, it had instructed clerks to check their stocks and remove any faulty panes. No more would be found, but at the time, Robey had no way of knowing that.

Postal inspectors visited Robey's apartment later the same evening, but he had not yet returned home. They waited outside for a while, then left. Robey, apparently fearing just such an eventuality, had ridden around on a streetcar after leaving Colman's office, waiting until after dark to come home. Robey and his wife spent an anxious night with the pane of inverted Jennies tucked under their mattress.

Again the following day, a postal inspector visited Robey at work, insisting once more that he surrender the stamps. Robey again refused. Pressure from the postal inspectors together with the possibility that other panes might be discovered crystallized Robey's decision to sell the stamps as quickly as possible. He sent telegrams to several out-of-town dealers, among them Elliot Perry of Westfield, New Jersey, and Percy Mann of Philadelphia. Perry didn't have a feel for the value of the pane; Mann came to Washington, viewed the pane, and offered $10,000 for it, which Robey declined. Three days after he had discovered the pane, Robey decided to go to New York City to try his luck.

On May 17, Robey took a train to New York. First he stopped at the office of Colonel Edward H. R. Green, the eccentric multi-millionaire collector, but Green was out of town. Next, he talked to dealers at Stanley Gibbons, Ltd. and at Scott Stamp and Coin Company, and he talked to John Klemann of Nassau Stamp Company, but couldn't make a deal with any of them. None thought the stamps were worth anywhere near the $10,000 Percy Mann had offered.

Discouraged, Robey telephoned Mann from New York that night, told him that no one had matched his offer, but that he had decided to keep the pane rather than sell it. However, Mann was not about to give up. He kept talking and finally persuaded Robey to stop in Philadelphia to see him on his way to Washington the next day. When Robey arrived in Philadelphia, Mann introduced him to Eugene Klein, who was a well-known local dealer. Klein asked Robey to name his price. Robey replied that he'd have to get at least $15,000. Klein didn't object to the price, but wanted a twenty-four-hour option to buy the pane. Robey thought it over for a moment, then agreed. Klein would have until three o'clock the following day to buy the pane for $15,000.

Robey returned to Washington, perhaps sorry he had not asked for more money. It is reported that Hamilton Colman offered Robey $18,000 upon his return, but that Robey couldn't accept because of Klein's option. In any case, Klein telephoned the next day to exercise his option, requesting that Robey appear at his office in Philadelphia the following day to close the deal. The next morning Robey, accompanied by his father-in-law, boarded the train to Philadelphia with a shoe box clutched under his arm. The pane of inverted Jennies was inside. At Klein's office, Robey handed over the shoebox in return for a cashier's check for $15,000. Robey had made a $14,976 profit in less than a week.

Klein had used his twenty-four-hour option to arrange a sale for the invert pane to Colonel Green, the same Colonel Green Robey had attempted to see on his trip to New York. Green, who had a special weakness for inverts, agreed to pay $20,000 for the pane, a quick $5,000 profit for Klein.

Klein also worked out an arrangement with Green to sell surplus copies of the invert, first for $250 each, which Klein split $225/$25 with Green, and later for $350 each, which he split $225/$125 with Green. Green suggested that Klein keep the extra $100 when the price rose to $350. With an income estimated at more than $2 million a year, Green apparently wasn't concerned with a few hundred dollars. Green kept the choice pieces: the center line block, the plate block of eight, an arrow block, and the lower left margin block. Klein sold a fair number of Green's surplus inverts, although at the time of Green's death in 1936, forty-one copies remained in the colonel's possession. When Green's four key pieces were auctioned, the plate block realized $27,000; the center line block, $22,000; the lower left corner block, $17,000; and the arrow block, which had been broken into pairs, $13,750; a total of $79,500, nearly four times the original cost of the entire pane.

Those who bought inverted Jennies early got in on the ground floor. In the years that followed, prices rose whenever inverts came to market. A single copy sold in 1969 for $33,000. Eight years later the same stamp sold for $62,500. In 1978, the inverted Jenny broke the $100,000 mark for a single stamp. Less desirable copies sold for less, as little as $65,000—still enormous appreciation over their original cost. The stamp market exploded in the late 1970s and with it, the price of inverts. In 1982 at the peak of the market, a select copy realized $198,000 ($180,000 plus $18,000 buyer's premium) in Robert A. Siegel's Rarities of the World sale. Since then, prices for inverts have stabilized at a lower, but still stratospheric level of $100,000 to $125,000.

William T. Robey won the post office lottery. Over the decades others, too, have won the post office lottery. Everyone who buys stamps plays, and the payoff can be huge, if you know what to look for. More about that in "Errors on Stamps."

FAMOUS COLLECTORS

Count Philippe von Ferrari is regarded as the greatest stamp collector who ever lived. Born in France in 1848 of wealthy parents, Ferrari was a sickly, fragile child. His mother introduced him to stamps when he was ten years old, hoping they would entertain him and take his mind off his troubles. The intricately printed bits of paper fascinated young Ferrari. Almost immediately, he decided that he would own a copy of every stamp ever issued, and he never wavered from that goal. By the time he was in his thirties, Ferrari had amassed the most complete collection then known. Along the way, he had inherited one of the greatest fortunes in Europe, which simplified the task. He spent millions of French francs on stamps, seeking out individual rarities as well as buying intact some of the finest collections in the world.

Count Ferrari

In 1878 Ferrari acquired the unique British Guiana one-cent magenta for approximately $700, a lot of money in those days. He acquired every rarity he encountered without hesitation, allowing his philatelic curator, Pierre Mahe, a budget of 50,000 francs per week to buy stamps. At one point, Ferrari's relatives, thinking he was crazy for "squandering" so much money on stamps, went to court to stop him. The judge decided that Ferrari's behavior might be eccentric but not insane. Ferrari zealously continued his quest for stamps until his death in 1917.

Ferrari never exhibited his collection or showed it to anyone except his philatelic curators. He bought and bought and bought, just salting away his purchases.

In all, Count Ferrari devoted fifty-six years of his life to collecting stamps. After his death, his magnificent collection was disbursed in a series of fourteen sales held between 1921 and 1925. The Ferrari auctions attracted bidders from all over the world, either in person or represented by agent. Bidders constituted a veritable who's who of philately: Alfred Caspery, Maurice Burrus, King George V of Great Britain, Alfred Lichtenstein, and Arthur Hind. The combined sales yielded $1,428,000, an astronomical sum of money at the time.

King George V of Great Britain, who reigned from 1910 to 1936, was also an avid collector and a philatelic scholar as well. Unlike Ferrari, George V did not attempt to obtain every stamp in the world. He specialized in stamps of the British Empire and formed a magnificent collection of stunning quality and comprehensiveness, which included proofs, specimens and artwork—every conceivable item the resources of the monarchy could bring to bear on the quest. The king's collection lacked only one item for completion, the unique British Guiana one-cent magenta, which came to market during the series of Ferrari auctions. George V sent an agent to bid on the stamp, but the extravagant and boorish American textile manufacturer, Arthur Hind, outbid him. Hind paid $32,500 for the one-cent magenta, the highest price ever paid for a single postage stamp at the time. It's been rumored—but never confirmed—that Hind offered the rarity

King George V of Great Britain.

to George V as a gift, but the king declined. Later, during a visit to Buckingham Palace at the invitation of the kind, Hind had the audacity to boast to George V that his—Hind's—collection was better than the king's.

Rumor also has it—again, unconfirmed—that a second copy of the one-cent magenta surfaced later, that Hind bought it and then burned it, so that his copy would continue to be unique.

Hind was neither a philatelic scholar nor a particularly meticulous collector. When Hind's collection came to market after his death, the philatelic world was horrified to discover that he had mounted stamps with adhesive tape, with poor-quality glue or anything else handy, without the slightest thought to the damage they would cause. As a result, many priceless rarities were permanently discolored or disfigured and when auctioned sold for far less than they might otherwise have.

Unlike the Ferrari and Hind collections, George V's remained intact after his death, and today resides in Buckingham Palace, part of the Royal Philatelic Collection. Each successive monarch, including Queen Elizabeth II, has added to it.

Other prominent stamp collectors include William H. Crocker (1861-1937), the California banker and financier; Alfred Caspery (1868-1955), investment banker; Josiah K. Lilly, Jr. (1893-1966), the pharmaceutical magnate; Theodore Steinway (1883-1957) of piano manufacturing fame; King Farouk of Egypt (1920-1965); President Franklin D. Roosevelt (1882-1945); and Colonel Edward H.R. Green (1868-1936), son of the fabulously wealthy Hetty Green, just to name a few.

Colonel Edward H.R. "Ned" Green is best remembered for having purchased the intact sheet of inverted Jennies in 1918. Green did not take up stamp collecting until midlife, when, so the story goes, he bought a packet of stamps for a friend's son in 1916 at the Scott Stamp and Coin Co. in New York and liked them so much he kept them. So smitten was he, that he returned the following day and bought $31,000 more.

Ned's mother, Hetty Green, the infamous "Witch of Wall Street," had amassed a fortune worth $100,000,000, but was a miser of unrivaled proportion. She made a home for her two children, Ned and Sylvia, in a coldwater flat in Hoboken, New

Jersey, that rented for less than $20 a month when she could easily have afforded better. At the time, she owned several thousand real estate properties and had tens of millions of dollars outstanding in short-term loans and mortgages, all at high interest rates. Yet she dressed in cheap clothes, worked in an unheated office, warmed her lunch of oatmeal on the radiator of a neighboring office, and haggled over the price of everything, including groceries.

When young Ned injured his leg in a sledding accident, Hetty dressed him in ill-fitting clothes and took him to the Bellevue Hospital Free Clinic for treatment. A few days later, when the staff learned Hetty's identity, they demanded payment, which she refused. Instead, she bundled Ned up, took him home, and treated his leg with poultices and patent medicine. His leg was never right after that and a few years later doctors had to amputate it above the knee. Green was forced to walk with a wooden leg for the rest of his life.

Upon Hetty's death in 1916, Ned and his sister Sylvia inherited the fortune. Ned set about spending his share with as much enthusiasm as his mother had displayed accumulating it. He built a million-dollar mansion, staffed it with more than a hundred employees, bought the biggest yacht in the world, built his own private airfield, and bought a radio station, which he ordered to play nothing but music he liked. Green stood six feet four inches and weighed more than 275 pounds. He was a large man with large appetites. During the course of the next twenty years he ate, drank, caroused, and collected with gusto, amassing one of the largest hoards of stamps ever assembled.

The stamps he accumulated, purchased both singly and in collections, ranged from the common to the rare and elusive. There seemed to be no rhyme or reason to his acquisitions. Unlike other great collectors who became philatelic scholars, connoisseurs or highly focused collection builders, Green remained the consummate acquisitor, buying whatever struck his fancy, then promptly forgetting he owned it. He lacked both discipline and focus, but never seemed to be aware of it. He loved errors above all other kinds of stamps, which led him to purchase the pane of Jenny inverts, as well as more than a dozen of the rare 1969 inverts, dozens of the 1901 Pan American inverts, and 28 of the 49 known complete sheets of the imperforate 5-cent color error of 1917.

Green died in 1936. Eight years later, his massive hoard came to market. In terms of sheer bulk, it was the largest holding of stamps ever to come to market, amounting to more than 50,000 lots spread over 28 auctions held between 1942 and 1946. At the time Green's collection was broken up, it still contained 41 of Green's original purchase of 100 Jenny inverts. The series of 28 auction sales yielded more than $1,800,000, which should be multiplied by at least a factor of ten to get an idea of value in current dollars.

King Farouk of Egypt was another large man with large appetites. Before being deposed in 1952, the arrogant and

King Farouk

egotistical monarch enjoyed not only enjoyed the singular advantage of being able to order his own likeness on postage stamps, but also of having proofs, imperforates and other rarities created whenever the whim moved him, which was often. Farouk squandered money on a lavish life-style—parties, travel, automobiles, jewels, mistresses—at a time when most Egyptians scraped along at subsistence levels. After Egypt came out on the short end in the war with Israel in 1948, the military began to grumble, and in 1952, fed up with Farouk's extravagance and ineptitude, deposed him. The playboy king settled in Monaco, where he continued his opulent lifestyle until an early death at age forty-five in 1965.

President Franklin D. Roosevelt is perhaps the best-known American stamp collector. He took up stamp collecting as a boy and continued collecting throughout his life, taking an active role in the decision-making process for all stamps issued during his administration. Roosevelt appointed his campaign manager and long-time political advisor, James A. Farley, postmaster general. Together they had a ball with stamps, and so did the stamp collectors of America. Farley seemed to enjoy philately, or at least the publicity surrounding it, as much as FDR enjoyed collecting.

Franklin D. Roosevelt.

Farley loved staging media events, making a big show of autographing the first sheet of stamps off the press for his friend President Roosevelt, basking in the glare of newsreel camera lights, energized by the staccato bursting of flashbulbs.

Farley gave press sheets to his friends as well. When one of Farley's friends tried to pledge his uncut, imperforate, ungummed press sheet as collateral for a loan of several thousand dollars—pointing out to the loan officer that imperforate sheets could not be obtained by the public and were therefore very valuable—collectors cried foul. FDR's political enemies jumped on the bandwagon. The public was outraged that the postmaster general appeared to be profiting from his position, to the tune of thousands of dollars—a fortune at the time, which was during the Depression. Most Americans earned less than $50 a month and considered themselves lucky just to have a job. Congress finally forced Farley to make the ungummed, imperforate stamps available to the public. Ironically, in reissuing them the post office reaped an enormous dividend. The demand for "Farley's Follies" translated into more than $1,500,000 in sales, most if it pure profit because few of the stamps ever saw postal duty.

No one ever suggested that President Roosevelt requested special stamps or special treatment. Evidence suggests that Farley, not a collector himself, actually distributed the press sheets as souvenirs, unaware they would be worth a lot of money or that anyone would consider it improper.

FDR brought a keen sense of philatelic aesthetics and American history to the stamps issued during his presidency. He believed United States postage stamps should possess dignity and merit. He vetoed subjects he felt were not worthy of honoring on postage stamps. The more than 200 stamps issued during his twelve-year

Examples of stamps issued during Roosevelt's administration.

presidency include some of the most beautiful, well-designed stamps ever issued by the United States. They celebrate the simple egalitarian majesty of our culture and possess a quality of unassuming nobility that American stamps have not exhibited since.

ERRORS ON STAMPS

Everyone who buys stamps plays the post office lottery whether they know it or not. If you're lucky enough to find a roll of stamps without perforations, don't take it back and complain. Don't cut the stamps apart; instead, contact an error dealer. You may have just won the post office lottery.

Today, stamp production is nearly one hundred percent automated. The touch of the button starts a press the size of a freight car rolling, an enormous roll of paper begins turning, and stamps flow out the other end, printed, perforated, and packaged—never touched by human hand, never seen by human eye. When humans performed quality control inspections, few errors escaped their vigilance. Today, with billions of stamps being printed every year, it's simply not feasible for humans to perform quality inspections. Machines do it—almost as well as humans but not quite. Errors slip out—not many, just a few of the billions and billions of stamps printed every year. So few as to be statistically insignificant to a quality control analyst. But those few are prized by collectors, who value them for their odd appearance and rarity.

Major errors are the most valuable kinds of errors. They can be worth more than $100,000 (in cases such as the inverted Jenny), but the vast majority reside in the $100 to $5,000 range. A major error is defined as the complete omission of perforations, the complete omission of one or more colors on a multicolored stamp, the inversion of one of the printed elements of the design, or a stamp printed in the wrong color.

In order to be considered an imperforate error, all traces of perforations between stamps must be absent (including faint impressions that do not break the paper, known as blind perfs). In order to be considered a color-omitted error, the color(s) described as omitted must be *completely* omitted. Even a trace of color visible under magnification disqualifies a stamp from being considered a color-omitted error.

The term "major error" is used to distinguish the foregoing from stamps with minor production imperfections, which are known as EFOs (errors, freaks, and oddities). Multitudes of EFOs exist, and include items such as misperfs (perforations shifted into the design or away from it), foldovers (stamps containing paper inadvertently folded back on itself during printing), ink smears, over- or underinking, and color shifts (one or more colors out of register). Most EFOs are worth from $5 to $75, although some of the more spectacular ones sell for as much as several hundred dollars. But by and large, EFOs are quite affordable and well within the reach of most collectors.

Stamps containing design errors (such as the wrong number of stars on a flag) are generally not considered errors in the philatelic sense (unless a corrected version is released and the term "error" is used to distinguish the two), and have no particular value above and beyond their ordinary value.

Imperforate coil pair.

The most commonly encountered major error is the imperforate coil stamp. The value of imperforate coil stamps ranges from a few dollars per pair to more than a thousand per pair, depending on rarity. Generally, imperforate sheet stamps are more valuable than imperforate coil stamps because fewer are discovered. And of the sheet stamps, imperforate commemoratives are usually more valuable than imperforate definitives, again because fewer tend to be discovered. The foregoing comments are generalizations and exceptions exist. With regard to errors, the final arbiter of value is rarity.

Emily Dickinson commemorative with color omitted (left); normal (right).

Generally—but not always—stamps with a color or colors omitted are worth more than imperforates because they are discovered less frequently, they tend to surface in smaller quantities, and they tend to be more visually striking. And given comparable scarcity, the more visually striking a color-omitted error, the more valuable. Color-omitted errors can be very subtle, so check stamps carefully. Collectors and dealers are generally suspicious of used stamps that purport to have colors omitted because used stamps are susceptible to bleaching and chemical treatment. Stamps with chemically altered colors are known as changelings and have no philatelic value.

Inverts are rare. Since the United States began printing stamps in 1847, only twelve inverts have been discovered. The most famous is the inverted Jenny. The most recent U.S. invert, the $1 Rush Lamp and Flame with the flame inverted (discovered in 1986), has been selling in the $12,500 to $17,500 price range, which makes the aggregate value of the discovery (95 stamps) more than $1 million.

The value of a newly discovered error is never clear, either to the dealer or the finder, and ultimately depends on how many more like it surface—and how quickly. No absolute ratio of quantity to

Pan American invert (left); Rush Lamp flame invert (right).

price exists, but generally, a modern (post-1950) major error for which less than twenty-five are known sells for thousands of dollars; for which less than a couple hundred are known sells for hundreds; and for which more than a thousand are known sells for less than $25. There are exceptions, but you can see how quickly price falls as quantity rises. Classic major errors sell for more than modern major errors of comparable quantity, by virtue of their age, their charisma, and long market history.

Finders of major errors face a dilemma: hold out for top dollar and hope no more surface, or take what the market offers and eliminate the risk. The value of an initial discovery diminishes in proportion to the magnitude of additional discoveries. Dealers, too, face a dilemma: offer a high price to beat out competition and pray no more surface, or sit on the sidelines and wait for the market to sort itself out.

The answer is never clear and usually depends on buyer's and seller's perception of the odds. A roll of 100 imperforate definitive flag stamps contains 50 pairs (imperforates are collected in pairs or multiples because ostensibly imperforate singles can be easily created by trimming perforations off normal stamps). Flag definitives usually have an extended life, often several years during which time many billions are printed. Experience has shown that not only do definitive coils invariably show up imperforate, but that over time they show up in large numbers.

Commemorative imperforates are much scarcer because they are printed in small quantities and remain on sale for only a limited time. The same is true for commemorative color-omitted errors.

The risk of additional quantities of a newly discovered color-omitted commemorative surfacing is much less, but not zero.

In 1986, the initial discoverer of the AMERIPEX booklet—a commemorative booklet—with black omitted sold his find for $500 per booklet. Ten more booklets surfaced within a week and the buy price dropped to $250 per booklet. Shortly thereafter, 100 more turned up and the price plummeted to $75. Then 300 more surfaced, then 500 more, and the price sank to $35 per booklet, then $20, and finally $15. Within the next few weeks, thousands more surfaced, and sellers found their error booklets difficult to move at any price. The market for AMERIPEX black-omitted error booklets had fallen apart in less than ten days.

Conversely, when about 25 pairs of the non-denominated "C" coil stamp turned up imperforate in 1981, dealers were reluctant to offer much for it because odds favored more coming to market. The "C" coil was, after all, a definitive, albeit a non-denominated transitional one, and dealers knew than hundreds of millions had been printed. The discoverer estimated the pairs to be worth $750 to $1,000 each. Dealers declined to buy, confident that more would surface, possibly hundreds or even thousands of pairs. And they knew that if that happened, the "C" coil could easily end up a $10 pair. So the owner kept the stamps. Time passed. No more imperforate "C" coil stamps turned up until years later, and then only a handful. The "C" coil is one of the rarest modern imperforate coils, and sells for about $1,000 per pair. Newly discovered major errors present risks for buyer and seller alike.

TIP: Don't make too much noise if you find an error. Rumors fly in the stamp business. A chance remark about a newly discovered error passing enough pairs of lips leaves the impression that many more of the error exist than actually do. That impression can only have a negative impact on dealers' perception of value and the size of their offers. Be discreet in your inquiries. Initially, contact one or two dealers specializing in error stamps, and go from there. *Top Dollar Paid: The Complete Guide to Selling Your Stamps* contains a more complete discussion on strategies for selling newly discovered major errors.

If you're interested in error stamps, look into the Errors, Freaks, Oddities Collectors Club (EFOCC). The cost is nominal and the club journal alone is worth the price of membership.   The *Catalogue of Errors on U. S. Postage Stamps* lists and prices all known U.S. major errors, including quantities known for most. It will give you a good feel for the relationship between quantity and price, as well as make you aware of what to watch for.

Over the decades, hundreds of new major errors have been discovered by keen-eyed individuals who knew what to look for. Next time you buy a roll of stamps or a booklet, consider for a moment that you have a lottery ticket in your hand. The odds of winning are slim, but if you do, the payoff can be great. And the best part is that if you lose, you can use the stamps on mail just as you intended, and it cost you nothing to play!

FAKES & FORGERIES

The terms "counterfeit," "fake," "forgery," and "bogus" are applied to stamps that are not legitimate. Fakes are not much of a problem for the general or casual collector buying moderately priced stamps, still you should be aware that the problem exists. Cheap stamps are seldom faked, and when they are, the work is often crude and easy to spot. The most dangerous and deceptive fakes are most often encountered where real money is involved, and there the buyer needs to beware. This overview will make you aware of what to look for and what to avoid. Several excellent books on the subject exist and are mentioned in the text below.

FAKES

Faking is nothing new. Many fakes were created decades ago, so the fact that a stamp has been in a collection for fifty years has little bearing on its genuineness.

Postal Counterfeits. Counterfeits manufactured to defraud the post office are rare. Apparently, those willing to risk jail for counterfeiting prefer printing currency. In fact, postal counterfeits are so rare that they're usually worth more than their genuine counterparts. The allies counterfeited German stamps during World War II for use on propaganda mail dropped inside the Third Reich. These, too, are prized by collectors and worth far more than their genuine counterparts.

Philatelic Forgeries. These are known as forgeries rather than counterfeits because they are intended to defraud collectors rather than a postal service.

A number of master craftsmen (and more than a few talented amateurs) produced dangerous forgeries of classic foreign stamps during the nineteenth century and early twentieth century. They concentrated on rare, elusive, or expensive issues. Your risk of getting a classic forgery is small unless you're buying individual big-ticket stamps, in which case you should insist on an expert certificate with every stamp.

Reproductions and Reprints. You're much more likely to come across a reproduction or reprint than an out-and-out forgery. During the early days of the hobby, dealers routinely sold reprints and reproductions of rare stamps, which they advertised as such. There was no intent to defraud. In fact, one dealer ad urged collectors not to waste money on expensive originals when they could fill albums spaces with excellent reproductions at little cost. Initially, no one thought there was anything wrong with making and selling reproductions and reprints. As the hobby grew more sophisticated, the philatelic community began to frown on the practice, and eventually it stopped.

Reprints and reproductions still turn up in old-time albums. They're known as album weeds because of the frequency with which they show up. Reproductions of nineteenth-century stamps of the Roman States are endemic—and often encountered in sets in uncharacteristically good condition. Sets of genuine Roman States stamps are worth thousands; the reproductions have little value. So, before you celebrate finding $10,000 worth of rare stamps, make sure they're not reproductions.

TIP: Old stamps usually show their age. Be suspicious of any nineteenth-century stamp that looks too good to be true. And be doubly suspicious of nineteenth-century sets (especially expensive ones) containing stamps of uniform high quality. They're probably reproductions.

Catalogues warn about which issues to watch out for and provide tips on how to identify many bogus stamps.

**The fake coil at right was trimmed from a sheet stamp
similar to that at left.**

Fake Coils. Coils are among the most frequently faked U.S.
stamps. Expensive coil stamps are faked by trimming perforations
off parallel sides of an inexpensive sheet stamp of the same design.
Fakes are usually narrower than genuine coils; the trimmed sides
are often not parallel; and traces of perforations often remain
visible on carelessly trimmed edges.

The rare 1902-1903 definitive coils are frequently faked (as
illustrated above) and should never be purchased without an expert
certificate.   Fake coils of the Washington-Franklin series are
endemic. *The Expert's Book*, by Paul Schmid is the best book on
Washington-Franklin fakes and how to spot them. Later coils are
seldom faked because they're neither rare nor expensive.

Line pairs (lines appear on rotary press coils where the printing
plates were joined, about every 24 stamps or so) are sometimes
faked by adding a line with a pen and ruler. Faked line pairs are
seldom encountered and usually only on expensive issues. Fake
lines are usually easy to spot. The ink used to make the line often
does not quite match that of the stamp, and a genuine line rises
above the surface of the paper due to the nature of intaglio
printing. You can feel it with your finger. Lines added by pen are
perfectly smooth.

Expensive booklet panes are sometimes created by trimming
perforations off less expensive sheet stamps.   Trimming off
perforations usually leaves abnormally small margins, a sure sign
of tampering. Make sure booklet panes have large margins on their
straight-edged sides.

This German stamp is worth less than $20 mint; but $3,000 to $4,000 with genuine cancel.

Fake Cancels. In some cases, catalogue value for a used stamp is the same as or more than a mint example. A heavily hinged mint stamp (worth only a small fraction of catalogue because of its disturbed gum) can be transformed into very fine used copy by soaking off the disturbed gum and applying a light cancel. The resulting "problem free" used stamp is worth double or triple the impaired mint stamp.

Generally, the greater the disparity in price between used and mint—when a used stamp catalogues more than a mint stamp—the more suspicious you should be.

Fake cancels and ancillary markings are sometimes added to increase the value of a cover. Stamps are sometimes added to stampless covers and tied with fake cancels, or low-denomination stamps lifted off and replaced with high denominations, which are rare on cover and worth much more on cover than off cover. Nineteenth-century covers are the usual targets for this type of trickery, and specialists the ones most often at risk because they are the primary market for rare covers.

Check cancels carefully on expensive covers. Many fakes are surprisingly obvious if you just pay attention. Be aware that fakes exist, but don't begin to worry that every item is a fake.

Fake Errors. Imperforate singles are easily faked by trimming perforations off perforated copies, especially those with jumbo margins. That's why no one collects imperforate singles.

Fake used color-omitted errors are most often created by bleaching or exposing stamps to chemical treatment. Collectors generally ignore even genuine used color-omitted errors. They sell for little. Only a few mint color-omitted errors have ever been faked because exposure to chemical agents affects gum and makes them easy to spot. The Copernicus commemorative of 1973 with yellow omitted is one of the few that has been successfully faked. An expert certificate is essential when buying this stamp. Stamps whose color has been altered (as opposed to removed) by chemical treatment are known as changelings, and have no philatelic value.

Catalogues generally warn about issues susceptible to faking, so read footnotes carefully before buying.

Overprints and Surcharges. Overprints and surcharges are sometimes faked to turn inexpensive stamps into expensive varieties. Cheap stamps with overprints are seldom faked.

In the late 1920s, rural post offices in Kansas and Nebraska suffered a rash of burglaries. To make it more difficult to sell elsewhere stamps stolen in those states, the postal service overprinted then current definitives with either "Kans." or "Nebr." The experiment didn't have much impact on the thefts, and the postal service abandoned it after a short time. Kansas-Nebraska overprints were scarce from the beginning and fakes started turning up right away.

Stamps of the Kansas-Nebraska issue with genuine overprints.

Fake Kansas-Nebraska overprints most often appear on used stamps because the raw material (unoverprinted definitives) is abundant and cheap. Most Kansas-Nebraska fakes are laughably amateurish and easy to spot. Genuine overprints were applied by printing press. Fakes are frequently rubber stamped or typewritten. Stamp pad ink is more grayish than the solid black printer's ink, and the hole left by a typed period is a dead giveaway. Fakers also make the mistake of overprinting the wrong perforation variety.

Genuine Kansas-Nebraska overprints always gauge perf 10½x11, not perf 10 or perf 11.

The easiest way to spot fakes of any kind is by comparison with genuine examples. Fakers can never precisely match the subtleties of an original. Pay attention to catalogue footnotes that warn of fake overprints.

IMPROVEMENTS

It may be perfectly respectable, even desirable, to restore fine art or vintage automobiles, but not stamps. Improvements, or any other alteration, are the kiss of death in philately. The premiums commanded by high-quality stamps are the reason many off-quality stamps are "improved."

Regumming. A regummed stamp has had new gum applied to simulate its original gum. Regumming is a fact of life. Buyers should be aware of the risk, but not intimidated by it. The attempt is often clumsy and amateurish, easy to spot with a little practice. However, clever and dangerous regumming jobs exist, especially coming out of Europe, where gum is applied by airbrush and other sophisticated techniques. Skilled regumming jobs are difficult to detect except by professionals who handle stamps every day, but most are easy to spot if you know what to look for.

If you suspect a stamp has been regummed, compare its gum with gum on other stamps of the same series. One- or two-cent denominations make good comparison specimens because they are rarely regummed. Regummers usually concentrate their efforts on expensive higher denominations. If the gum on your suspect stamp looks markedly different that the gum on your comparison specimen, beware. Unevenly applied gum, thinly applied gum, gum speckled with dust or tiny air bubbles, are all indications of regumming.

All unused nineteenth-century stamps should be examined for regumming, *especially* if offered as *never hinged.* The vast majority of so-called never-hinged nineteenth-century U.S. stamps have been regummed. Be extremely cautious of expensive stamps, especially high values of the Columbian and Trans-Mississippi series. Some regummed stamps have even been lightly hinged to throw buyers off. Regumming is seldom encountered on stamps issued after 1920. It's not much of a problem for the worldwide generalist or the collector of low or moderately priced stamps.

The best protection is to buy from a reliable source, especially if you're buying expensive stamps. Regumming is only a problem if you're not aware of it. Learn to spot signs of tampering. Insist on expert certificates with expensive stamps. And don't be afraid to ask a dealer what to look for. They're usually happy to show you, and one look is worth a thousand words.

Reperforating. A reperforated stamp has had perforations added to simulate original perforations. This is done either to improve centering (infrequently) or get rid of a straightedge (frequently). Collectors disdain straight-edged stamps so much that they typically sell for only 10 or 20 percent of catalogue. Hence the incentive to make a stamp more salable and increase its value by adding perforations.

Reperforating is most often encountered on stamps that were issued in sheets with straight edges on one or two sheet margins, such as the Columbian Exposition issue of 1893 and the Trans-Mississippi issue of 1898. Stamps issued in panes without straightedges are rarely reperforated.

Again, half the battle is just being aware of the problem. A stamp's perforations consists of two elements: the size of the hole and the spacing between the holes. Reperforators often get the spacing between holes right, but not the size of the hole. Experienced collectors test a suspect stamp by laying it atop a known genuine example (an inexpensive one- or two-cent value from the same set works well). Compare the perforations. If they don't match, the stamp's likely been reperforated. Be suspicious of any stamp with a row of flat perforation tops, which are typically created when punching holes along an otherwise straight edge. Normal teeth are somewhat roughened when stamps are pulled apart, not left flat as if cut by scissors. Again, ask a dealer to demonstrate techniques for spotting reperforated stamps, and get a copy of *How to Detect Damaged, Altered, and Repaired Stamps,* by Paul Schmid. It's one of the best books on "improvements." Profusely illustrated, it covers regumming, reperforating, and other alterations in detail. It's inexpensive and every serious collector should own a copy.

Other Improvements. Be alert for thins. They're often visible to the naked eye; however, small subtle thins may only be visible when held up to light or dipped in watermark fluid. When held up to light, thin spots appear lighter than surrounding paper. When dipped in watermark fluid, thin spots appear darker than surrounding paper. Watch out for filled thins, i.e., thins that have been touched up with a paste of paper fibers, often applied with an artist's brush. Filled thins usually show up a different shade of white or as opaque spots when dipped in watermark fluid. Some stamps have been regummed over filled thins. These thins, too, show up in watermark fluid.

Watch out for ironed-out creases. Although often invisible to the naked eye, they're easy to spot in watermark fluid, showing up as dark lines. Pay attention to corner creases, which are often so small as not to be noticed unless one is looking for them.

Be on the lookout for retouched scuffs and scrapes on the fronts of stamps. They're often hidden by the careful application of colored ink to the affected areas. They're easy to spot if you take the time to look.

Small tears are often repaired with a delicate adhesive such as egg white. You can usually spot them with the naked eye or in watermark fluid.

In philately, the term "cleaned" refers to a stamp that's had its cancellation removed. Early nineteenth-century stamps are the ones most often cleaned. Stamps are cleaned to increase their value, either by making them appear unused or, in the case of some pen-cancelled stamps, by recancelling them with device cancels (grids, circular date stamps, etc.), which are worth more than pen cancels. Fakers prefer pen-cancelled stamps for cleaning because writing ink is usually more susceptible to bleaching than stamp pad ink, and because pen-cancelled stamps are inexpensive compared to device-cancelled stamps. Sometimes bleached-out cancels show up in watermark fluid; however, ultraviolet light works better and in almost all cases reveals the tampering.

Improvements and faults are so often encountered on nineteenth-century stamps that it's reflexive for experienced collectors and dealers to hold them up to light or dip them in watermark fluid to check for problems.

EXPERT CERTIFICATES

Expert certificates are advisable for stamps prone to fakery and for expensive stamps. Stamps are expertized for authenticity, for gum and perforations, for use on cover, and for faults. You can request that a purchase be subject to confirmation by expert opinion. If the seller refuses, think twice. And when it comes time to sell, you'll find that dealers usually pay more for stamps with expert certificates, especially expensive varieties. *The Buyer's Guide: An Analysis of Selected U.S. Postage Stamps* advises—on stamp-by-stamp basis—when expertizing is necessary.

American Philatelic Expertizing Service expert certificate.

The Philatelic Foundation and the American Philatelic Expertizing Service are the two foremost expertizing bodies in the United States. Neither deals in stamps; they are impartial and their opinions highly respected throughout the philatelic community. Write for a submission form and fee schedule *before* sending a stamp to either service for an opinion. Both bodies issue certificates containing a color photograph of the subject stamp together with a summary of their findings. Fees are based on the value of the stamp (or cover), with a minimum fee applicable for items of nominal value or for items that turn out not to be genuine. Turn-around time is typically four to eight weeks. Consult the Resource Guide for their addresses.

Any discussion of fakes makes the problem sound worse than it is. Fakery most often afflicts expensive stamps, and most fakes can be spotted if one is reasonably attentive. Be alert, pay attention to catalogue cautions, be diligent in examining nineteenth-century stamps and those prone to fakery, and know when to expertize.

MARKET IN A NUTSHELL

The stamp market is more than 150 years old. It is broad and deeply rooted, with dealers spread across the world in most major cities and many small towns as well. They range in size from small mom-and-pop operations to publicly held corporations with multi-million dollar budgets, and they buy and sell stamps every day. As a result, stamps are highly liquid. American dealers are as close as the Yellow Pages, or if you live off the beaten path, the American Stamp Dealers Association (ASDA) maintains a no-fee referral service that will provide the addresses and telephone numbers of the dealers near you.

The stamp market is subject to all the economic factors that influence other markets: optimism and pessimism; inflation and deflation; boom and recession; interest rates, currency fluctuations, and speculation. Sometimes prices are strong; other times not. Over the long term, however, stamp prices (for high-quality material) rise and generally keep pace with inflation or beat it. Stamp values have increased about 500 percent in the last 50 years, or about ten percent per year.

The market for a nation's stamps is usually determined in the country of its origin. Developed nations with thriving economies have large, affluent collector bases and a strong market for their stamps. There is always a market for scarce, high-quality stamps of the United States, Western Europe, the British Commonwealth, and the Far East; and therefore, better potential for appreciation and stronger resale values.

On the other hand, there is usually little local domestic demand for stamps of undeveloped nations and tiny islands. Except for topicals sets and singles, demand is limited for stamps of Central and South America and for Africa—and prices for them are not as strong as for stamps of Western Europe and the Far East. The same can be said for the small island nations of the Caribbean and the Pacific, which export nearly 100 percent of the stamps they print.

More specifically, demand is strong for scarce, quality mint sets from Western Europe and the Far East, especially those of Germany, Japan, and China. During the desperate years immediately following World War II, collectors in former Axis countries could not afford to buy mint stamps, and collectors in other countries had little interest in stamps of their former enemies. Now an affluent generation of Germans and Japanese needs them, and prices for German and Japanese mint stamps of the postwar decade have risen sharply, and likely will continue to do so. Some (especially commemoratives and semi-postals) are scarce used and high priced too, but demand is not as great for them as for mint stamps.

Chinese stamps experienced a different problem during the cultural revolution of the late 1960s, but with a similar result. Party zealots condemned stamp collecting as a petty bourgeois pastime. The party churned out a steady stream of stamps praising Chairman Mao and the cultural revolution, but few were saved. Now that the Chinese are less dogmatic and more affluent, demand for Chinese stamps of all eras is growing rapidly.

Stamps of Vietnam are in demand both in the United States and abroad, as is postal history of the Vietnam war.

Stamps of Eastern Europe are in demand, too, now that the Soviet Union has disintegrated. Russian collectors are increasingly affluent and no longer fear owning czarist stamps.

And finally, mint never-hinged sets and singles of the world issued during the period 1930-1970 always seem to be in demand. Demand for hinged stamps of the period is also steady.

The stamp market is simply too broad to cover adequately here. The best way to keep up with what's going on is to read philatelic periodicals, and network with fellow collectors and stamp dealers.

Remarks such as "Japan's hot" or "Vatican's cooled down" (hypothetical remarks, by the way) tell the story. News about market trends spreads quickly.

Any discussion of the market inevitably raises the question of investment. Stamps do not possess some special, magical attribute for profit. As with any commodity, some stamps are good investments; many others are not. If you're buying stamps purely for investment, your success will be directly proportional to the amount of knowledge, homework, and experience you bring to the task.

Having said that, one of the advantages of philately is that when you've finished enjoying your collection, the stamps have residual value. That value should be regarded as a bonus, not the *raison d'être* for collecting. Ironically, it is often those collections built up over a lifetime by dedicated collectors with no particular thought to profit that prove to be the most profitable. Specialty collections carefully assembled by knowledgeable collectors contain the type of material in perennial demand by other advanced collectors—buyers with both the motivation and the money.

If you're buying for appreciation, concentrate on rarity and quality. There's always a demand for carefully formed collections of any nation or specialty containing balanced runs of premium stamps. The subject of stamp investing is covered more thoroughly in the book *Stamp Investing*. Refer to the Bibliography for more information.

GLOSSARY

adhesive: the gum used to attach a stamp to mail.

aerogramme: a lightweight type of postal stationery with gummed flaps that can be folded and sealed for mailing. Aerogrammes are intended primarily for international airmail correspondence.

aero-philately: the collecting of airmail stamps, covers, and related items.

airmail: a stamp intended primarily for use on airmail.

albino: usually occurring on a stamped envelope, and the result of the inked portion of the design failing to print, leaving only an impression of the uncolored embossed portion of the design.

album: a book in which a collection of stamps or covers is housed.

approvals: selections of stamps sent by mail, usually inexpensive singles or sets for the beginning or general collector. The collector purchases what he likes and returns the balance.

APO: army post office. *See* **FPO.**

APS: American Philatelic Society.

arrow block: a block of stamps on whose selvage appears an arrow-like marking that serves as a guide to assist printers in cutting press sheets apart at the time of production.

ASDA: American Stamp Dealers Association.

ATA: American Topical Association.

auxiliary marking: a mark placed on a cover explaining why it was handled in a certain way, e.g., "Return to Sender," "Postage Due," and the like.

backstamp: a postmark placed on the reverse of a cover to indicate its arrival date or time.

bank mixture: mixture of stamps on paper, so called because it traditionally originated from bank correspondence. Bank mixtures are regarded as premium mixtures because they contain a large number of high denomination and seldom encountered stamps.

BIA: Bureau Issues Association.

bicolor: a stamp printed in two colors.

bisect: a stamp cut in half (often diagonally) and used as one-half the face value of uncut stamp.

blind perforations: lightly impressed perforations that often give stamps the appearance of being imperforate. Stamps with blind perforations are not considered errors.

block: four or more unseparated stamps arranged in a rectangle.

BNA: British North America.

B-O-B: back of the book, includes stamps such as postage dues, special deliveries, parcel posts, etc., anything listed in the rear of the catalogue following definitives and commemoratives.

booklet pane: a small sheetlet of stamps bound between cardstock covers by staples, thread, or glue. Also, self-adhesive stamps sold in small panes that can be folded for carrying in purse or wallet.

bourse: a show in which dealers take booths and offer their wares to the stamp collecting public. Bourses are often held in conjunction with stamp shows or exhibitions.

broken set: a set of stamps missing some values; an incomplete set. *See* **short set.**

bullseye cancel: a cancellation, usually circular, struck squarely on the center of the stamp, also known as socked on the nose.

bureau precancel: a precancel whose city and state overprint was applied at the Bureau of Engraving and Printing. *See* **local precancel.**

cachet: pronounced ka-shay. A decorative illustration printed on a cover, usually in connection with the first day of issue of a new stamp or some other special event. Cachets may be printed, rubber stamped, hand painted, or applied by other means.

cancel: or cancellation. An obliterating mark applied to a stamp rendering it invalid for future use. Cancellations may be applied by hand stamp, machine, or pen. *See* **postmark.**

canceled to order (CTO): cancellations applied by governments, often to full sheets. CTOs are sold in bulk to packet makers, approval dealers, etc.

catalogue: a reference work that lists, illustrates, and prices postage stamps. Stamp catalogues can be general or specialized.

centering: the position of a stamp's design in relation to its perforations or to the edges of a stamp. Well-centered stamps possess even margins all around.

charity stamp: a semi-postal. *See* **semi-postal.**

cinderella: a general, all-encompassing term applied to any stamp-like item not valid for postage, such as exhibition labels, Christmas seals, and the like. Anything that looks like a postage stamp but is not.

CDS: circular date stamp. A circular postmark showing place of mailing together with date and in some cases, time.

classic: an early issue, usually nineteenth century.

cleaned: an item whose cancellation has been removed in order to make it appear uncancelled.

coil stamps: stamps issued in rolls. Coil stamps contain straight edges on two sides.

collateral material: material—often non-philatelic—related to stamps, covers, or postal history that provides additional insight or background to the items.

color changeling: a stamp whose normal color has been changed or eliminated by exposure to light or chemicals. Color changelings have no philatelic value.

comb perforation: perforations made by a device that punches three sides of a stamp at once, then three more, etc. *See* **harrow perforation** and **line perforation**.

combination cover: most often a cover containing stamps from two countries, usually the country of origin and the destination country. Also applied to first day covers that contain additional stamps related to the stamp being issued or to first day covers bearing both official and unofficial first day cancellations.

commercial cover: a cover used for business correspondence without any philatelic intent (although more recently any cover of a non-philatelic nature), as distinct from one created for a philatelic purpose. *See* **philatelic cover**.

commemorative: a special stamp issued to honor a special event, personality, anniversary, or topic, and typically available for a only limited time.

compact sheet: a pane of stamps containing fewer than the traditional 50 or 100 stamps—often 15 or 20 stamps—and often with decorative marginal inscriptions.

complete set: a set containing all of the stamps that comprise it.

compound perforations: perforations of two different gauges on the same stamp, such as perforated 10 on top and bottom and perforated 11 on either side.

computer vended postage: stamps dispensed by vending machines that imprint the denomination at the time the stamp is vended, usually on security paper containing a pre-printed background.

corner card: the return address on the upper left corner of a cover.

cover: philatelic term for an envelope, almost always implying that it has gone through the mail.

crash cover: a cover salvaged from an airplane crash or train wreck that has been forwarded to the addressee. Crash covers are usually marked by the postal service with an explanation explaining the delay.

cut cancel: a cancellation that cuts into the stamp, thus defacing it. Often encountered on documentary stamps.

cut square: a piece containing the postage imprint cut from postal stationery, usually to facilitate mounting in an album. *See* **entire.**

dead country: a country that no longer issues postage stamps, most often due to changing political reality, such as former colonies (Belgian Congo, Mozambique Company) or nations absorbed by other countries (East Germany, South Vietnam).

definitive: a stamp, usually part of a series, available over an extended period of time for use on everyday mail. Definitives are also known as regular issues.

demonetized: no longer valid for the payment of postage. United States stamps were demonetized at the outbreak of the Civil War and replaced by stamps with new designs in order to prevent stocks in Southern post offices from being used by the Confederacy.

denomination: the value imprinted on the stamp, such as one cent or one dollar.

documentary: a revenue stamp used to evidence payment of tax on documents such as mortgages and wills.

DPO: discontinued post office. A post office no longer in operation.

dry gum: non-glossy gum that is flat in appearance, as opposed to "wet" gum, which is glossy or shiny in appearance. Also referred to as matte gum or dull gum.

dry printing: an intaglio printing process utilizing low-moisture content paper. Most U.S. stamps prior to the mid-1950s were printed on paper with high moisture content, which was necessary to ensure receptivity to printing ink. The wet-print process was phased out in the 1950s after the appearance of dry-print presses capable of handling low-moisture content paper. Dry-printed stamps usually display a sharper, more crisp appearance than wet-printed stamps. *See* **wet printing.**

duck stamp: a waterfowl-hunting stamp.

duplex cancel: a postmark containing two elements: one giving the name of the location and date; the second an obliterating mark intended to cancel the stamp.

early use: a stamp used before its official first day of sale.

EKU: earliest known use. The earliest date a stamp is known to have been used.

embossed: a raised design impressed onto paper by an embossing die, most commonly on stamped envelopes.

entire: a complete, intact item of postal stationery.

error: usually refers to a stamp with a major production error, i.e., a stamp lacking perforations, a stamp with a design element inverted, or a stamp with a color or colors omitted. Minor production irregularities are known as EFOs. Stamps with design errors (such as the wrong number of stars on a flag) are generally not considered "errors."

EFO: errors, freaks and oddities. A term applied to stamps with random minor production irregularities such as misaligned perforations, freak perforations, printing offset on reverse, ink smears, and the like.

essay: an unadopted stamp design, either an entire design not used, or a design very similar to the issued design except for small modifications.

event cover—a cover postmarked to commemorate an event or anniversary, often with cachet; similar to a first day cover, but not marking the issuance of a stamp.

expert certificate: a certificate issued by an acknowledged expert or expertizing body attesting to the genuineness or non-genuineness of a stamp or cover.

expert mark: a mark of authentication placed on the reverse of a stamp or cover by a recognized expert.

expertize: to have a stamp examined by an acknowledged expert or expertizing body and have an opinion given.

exploded: refers to a booklet that has been dissembled into individual panes.

face value: a stamp's denomination.

facsimile: a reproduction of a stamp, most often a rare stamp, and usually offered or marked as such. Unlike fakes or forgeries, facsimiles are not intended to deceive.

fake: an outright forgery; also a stamp (or cover) that has been modified to improve its value or desirability with the intent to defraud a buyer.

fancy cancel: a cancellation featuring a pictorial device or geometric design.

fault: any defect affecting the appearance or integrity of a stamp such as a tear, cut, crease, thin, scrape, stain, scuff, fold, pin-hole, foxing, etc.

favor cancel: a cancellation applied to a stamp or cover as a favor by a postal employee, often on an item that might not normally have been used on mail or have gone through the mail, or with a postmarking device not normally used for the issue.

first day cover (FDC): a cover, usually cacheted, postmarked on the first day a stamp is officially available for sale.

first flight cover: a cover, usually cacheted, carried on the first flight of a new airmail route.

fiscal: a revenue stamp. Revenue stamps used for postage are called postal-fiscals.

foxing: rust colored discoloration caused by microorganisms.

FPO: fleet post office.

frame: the outer border surrounding the central design of a stamp. *See* **vignette.**

frank: a mark indicating that postage has been paid, or in the case of those granted the privilege (known as the franking privilege), that postage is free. Presidents and members of Congress have the franking privilege, as often do members of the military during time of war.

fugitive ink: ink susceptible to fading or change of color with exposure to light or chemicals. Also inks—especially aniline inks—that run or bleed when wetted, to discourage re-use.

granite paper: a type of security paper containing tiny filaments of colored paper intended to discourage counterfeiting.

grill: a waffle-like pattern impressed into some nineteenth-century stamps to break their paper fibers and make them more receptive to postmarking ink. Used to prevent the removal of cancellations and re-use of stamps.

gum breakers: ridges impressed by special rollers on sheets of stamps to counteract their tendency to curl, especially when exposed to humidity. They are visible on the backs of most rotary press stamps issued between the 1920s and 1960s.

gum skip: a space, often small, on which gum was omitted during its original application. Most often encountered on U.S. stamps of the 1910s and 1930s.

gutter: the space between two panes of stamps on a sheet.

hand cancelled: cancelled with a hand-held device as opposed to cancelled by machine. Also called hand stamped.

harrow perforation: perforations made by a device that perforates an entire sheet of stamps at one stroke. *See* **comb perforation** and **line perforation**.

heavily hinged (HH): hinged with strong glue that has disturbed gum or will disturb it when removed.

hinge: a stamp hinge. A small piece of paper or glassine used to attach a stamp to an album page.

imperforate: lacking perforations.

imprint: information imprinted on the selvage of a pane of stamps, such as the name of the printer, value of the stamps, and so forth.

inscription block: a block of stamps on whose selvage appears a printed inscription.

intaglio: a method of printing in which the design is engraved (recessed) into a metal plate. Ink fills the recesses and when printed forms small ridges, which can be detected by magnifying glass or by running a finger over the design and feeling the ridges.

international reply coupon (IRC): a coupon good for one single-rate surface letter stamp. Coupons may be purchased or redeemed in any Universal Postal Union member nation. Used to enable an individual in one country to send postage for a reply to an individual in another country.

invert: a stamp with an element of its design upside down in relation to the other elements of the design.

job lot: a mishmash consisting of just about anything, loose stamps, stamps on albums pages, covers, mixtures, mint sets, remainders, etc., often sold by the carton. Dealers often dispose of surplus, disorganized material in the form of job lots. Sometimes called a mystery lot.

joint issue: stamps of two (or more) countries featuring a similar design, issued in collaboration with one another specifically to commemorate something important to both.

killer cancel: a heavy mark, typically covering most of a stamp's design, rendering it nearly unrecognizable, hence "killing" it.

kiloware: mixture of stamps on paper sold by the pound or kilogram, hence the name kiloware. *See* **mixture.**

label: in the philatelic sense, anything that resembles a stamp but is not. *See* **cinderella.**

laid paper: paper containing rows of subtle parallel lines impressed during manufacture. The rows are often visible to the naked eye if held up to light, and invariably visible when immersed in watermark fluid.

lightly hinged (LH): hinged so that the hinge mark is barely noticeable.

line pair: a pair of coil stamps on which a line appears between stamps. On engraved, rotary-press coil stamps, lines are created by ink that fills the space where the curved plates join and is then printed in the same fashion as ink from recesses in an intaglio stamp design.

line perforation: perforations made one row at a time. *See* **harrow perforation** and **comb perforation.**

local precancel: a precancel whose city and state overprint was applied locally rather than at the Bureau of Engraving and Printing. *See* **bureau precancel.**

local stamp: a stamp issued by a private firm to evidence payment of a fee for conveyance of mail to the nearest post office.

manuscript cancel: handwritten cancellation, usually including the date and location of mailing.

meter stamp: a stamp printed by a postage metering machine such as those made by the Pitney-Bowes Company.

mint: an unused stamp with full original gum as issued by the post office. *See* **unused**.

maximum card: a post card bearing the same illustration or design as the stamp affixed to it and cancelled with first day or commemorative cancellation.

military stamp: a postage stamp used exclusively by military personnel.

mission mixture: an on-paper mixture of stamps so called because its traditional source was religious or charitable organizations, and usually containing a wide variety of foreign stamps.

mixture: an assortment of stamps, most often on paper and unsorted, containing a variety of stamps including duplicates, most often sold in bulk by the ounce, pound, or kilogram. *See* **kiloware**.

mounts: clear plastic pouches or sleeves used to protect stamps and attach them to album pages.

multiple: a group of two or more unseparated stamps, such as a block, pair, strip, or pane.

mute cancel: a postmark that lacks the name of the place of cancellation and in some cases, the date, e.g., double oval registry postmarks and some military field post postmarks.

never hinged (NH): a stamp that has never been hinged.

new issue: a newly issued stamp or set, often received by subscription either directly from a postal administration or from a stamp dealer.

obsolete: a stamp no longer available at the post office.

occupation stamp: a stamp issued for use in a country or territory overrun by another power, e.g., after World War II, the allies issued stamps for use in occupied Germany.

off center: a stamp whose design is poorly centered in relation to its perforations.

off paper: used stamps that have been soaked off paper. Most often applied to mixtures, which are sold either "on paper" or "off paper."

official stamp: a stamp valid for use only by a government agency and intended for use only on official mail.

omnibus issue: a group of stamps issued by several postal administrations to mark or commemorate a single theme or event, e.g., those issued by nations of the British Commonwealth to commemorate the coronation of Queen Elizabeth II.

on cover: stamp attached to a cover.

on paper: *See* **off paper**.

on piece: a stamp attached to a piece of paper torn or cut from an envelope or wrapper.

original gum (OG): gum applied to a stamp at the time of manufacture.

overprint: printing applied to stamps after regular production, typically to denote a special purpose (such as airmail), commemorate something, as a control measure, etc. *See* **surcharge**.

packet: typically a printed window envelope containing an assortment of stamps for the beginner or general collector.

packet material: common, inexpensive stamps.

pair: two unseparated stamps.

pane: a finished "sheet" of stamps as sold in post offices, as distinct from a press or production sheet, which usually contains multiple panes of stamps.

patriotic cover: a cover bearing a patriotic cachet or slogan, most often produced during time of war, especially during the Civil War and World War II.

pen cancel: a cancellation made by hand, usually an "X" or other mark to deface a stamp.

perforations: the series of holes punched between stamps to facilitate their separation. The size of the holes and spacing vary from issue to issue. Perforations are measured by a perforation gauge.

perfin: short for perforated initials. Refers to a stamp with initials or a design punched in it by a perforating device. Perfins are utilized by firms (most frequently) and governments (occasionally) as a control measure to prevent pilferage or unauthorized use.

permit imprint: printed indicia used by permit-holding bulk mailers to evidence payment of postage.

philatelic cover: a cover prepared and sent by or for a stamp collector, often with stamps or combinations of stamps not normally encountered on mail, such as complete sets of semi-postals. *See* **commercial mail**.

pictorial stamp: a stamp featuring a scene or topic rather than the portrait of an individual, numeral, coat of arms or the like. Pictorials are generally large and colorful.

plate block: a block of stamps with the printing plate number(s) appearing on the selvage.

plate number: a security number assigned to a printing plate by the printer for inventory and control purposes, and most often seen on United States issues. All sheets of stamps in a print run made from the same plate will share the same plate number.

plate single: a single stamp with selvage tab attached containing a plate number.

PNC: plate number coil. A coil stamp on which a small printing plate number appears at the bottom. Plate numbers appear at the bottoms of stamps at predetermined intervals such as every 24th or 52nd stamp.

post office seal: an adhesive seal used to re-seal letters opened in transit, either intentionally or inadvertently, such as an item damaged by sorting machinery.

postcard: a privately produced card without imprinted postage and usually containing a printed greeting or illustration on the reverse. *See* **viewcard.**

postal cancel: a cancellation showing that a stamp has been used to pay postage rather than revenue purposes.

postal card: a card with postage imprinted on it by the Postal Service.

postal stationery: stationery sold by a postal service usually, but not always, with imprinted postage. Postal stationery includes postal cards, stamped envelopes, and aerogrammes.

postally used: a stamp actually used for postage rather than cancelled to order or used for some other purpose such as revenue service.

postmark: an official marking (usually circular but can be any shape or in manuscript or most recently, sprayed-on dot-matrix style characters) applied to a piece of mail, most often indicating date and place of mailing.

postmaster's provisional: a stamp issued by a postmaster. Generally refers to those issued during the period between the enactment of uniform postage by Congress in 1845 and the first U.S. postage stamps in 1847.

precancel: a stamp cancelled prior to use either by printed or hand-applied marking, in the beginning with the name of a city and state between two parallel bars, but later with only parallel bars or with class of service between parallel bars. For use by permit-holding bulk mailers. *See* **service inscribed.**

press sheet: a sheet containing multiple panes of stamps just as it came off the press.

private treaty: an arrangement in which as stamp dealer acts in the capacity of agent for a seller, receiving a commission for his services.

proof: a trial impression made from a die or plate before regular production in order to check engraving, color, etc.

quadrille paper: paper printed with a background of horizontal and vertical lines forming a grid of small squares, often faintly imprinted. Quadrilled blank pages are often used by collectors who design their own album pages because the grid makes it easy to lay out a geometric arrangement.

regummed: a stamp that has had new gum applied to simulate its original gum.

reissue: a stamp printed from original plates and released subsequent to becoming obsolete. *See* **reprint**.

reperforated: a stamp that has had perforations add to a straight edge or to a perforated edge that has been trimmed in order to improve centering.

reprint: a stamp that has been printed from new plates (often distinguishable from the original plates) and released subsequent to having become obsolete. *See* **reissue**.

revenue: a stamp used to evidence payment of a tax or fee. Postage stamps are occasionally used as revenue stamps, most often abroad. Examples of revenues include tobacco tax stamps, silver tax, playing card tax, stock transfer tax, and the like. Revenues are often referred to as "fiscals" in other countries.

roulette: a philatelic term referring to a series of small slits applied between stamps to facilitate separation. The slits may appear in a straight line or in a other configurations such as serpentine or sawtooth pattern.

seal: in the philatelic sense, a stamplike item not valid for postage, and often sold for charitable purposes, such as Christmas seals or Easter seals. *See* **post office seal**.

RPO: railway post office.

secret mark: a small, difficult to detect engraver's mark applied to a design so that stamps printed by one source (such as the Continental Bank Note Company) could be distinguished from identical stamps printed by another source (such as the National Bank Note Company).

selvage: the marginal area surrounding a sheet or pane of stamps. Sometimes spelled selvedge.

semi-postal: a postage stamp for which only part of the purchase price applies toward postage; the balance is collected for some other purpose, often a charitable cause. Semi-postals are usually, but not always, denominated by two figures, the first applying toward postage, the second toward the other purpose, i.e., 50c+20c. Also called charity stamps.

series: a group of stamps, usually definitives, sharing a theme or motif, and often issued over a period of time ranging from months to years, and usually in use for a number of years.

service inscribed: a type of stamp used by bulk mailers on which the class of service is inscribed (printed) at time of production. Referred to as precancels by some, however, the printed inscription usually appears to be the part of the design rather than a cancellation.

set: two or more stamps sharing a similar theme, motif, or appearance, usually commemoratives, usually issued within a short period time, and usually, but not always, of different denominations.

se-tenant: two or more different stamp designs printed next to one another on a pane of stamps, a souvenir sheet, a booklet, or a coil.

shade: a stamp possessing a variation in color, often slight or subtle, from the color normally encountered on the issue.

short set: an incomplete set of stamps, usually comprised of only the lower denominations.

socked on the nose: *See* **bullseye cancel**.

sound: free of faults.

souvenir card: a card containing printed examples of stamps (or currency). Souvenir cards are usually issued in connection with a stamp show or philatelic event. Souvenir cards are produced by both the government and private entities. Stamps appearing on souvenir cards are not valid for postage.

souvenir sheet: a sheet, usually small, containing one or more stamps, usually bearing a commemorative marginal inscription, and usually issued for a special event or occasion such as a philatelic exhibition. Stamps in souvenir sheets are valid for postage.

space filler: a damaged or otherwise normally uncollectible copy of a stamp good for no other purpose than filling an album space until a collectible copy comes along. Often used to imply that a stamp has little or no value.

special handling stamp: a class of stamps, now obsolete, used to pay a fee that entitled parcel post items (fourth class mail) to be given the same priority as first class mail.

specialist: one whose collection is narrowly focused on a specific country, issue, stamp, or collecting interest.

specimen stamp: a sample rendered postally invalid by the application of an overprint, e.g., "specimen" or "sample."

spray-on marking: an ink-jet marking sprayed on by mail processing machinery to confirm the time and place a piece of mail passed through the system, usually appearing at top right on a cover.

stamped envelope: an envelope on which postage has been pre-printed. *See* **postal stationery.**

stampless cover: a cover sent through the mail without postage stamps, the payment of postage evidenced by handstamp or manuscript. Usually refers to covers prior to the advent of postage stamps.

strip: three or more unseparated stamps arranged side-to-side or end-to-end.

supplement: an installment of album pages to bring a loose-leaf album up to date, usually published annually.

surcharge: an overprint that changes the face value of a stamp or piece of postal stationery. *See* **overprint.**

tab: a piece of selvage attached to an individual stamp.

tagging: a luminescent coating applied to stamps during printing. Usually invisible to the naked eye, tagging can be observed under ultraviolet light. Tagging may cover all or part of a stamp.

tête-bêche: pronounced tet-besh. Two adjacent stamps, one of which is inverted in relation to the other. From the French head-to-foot.

thematic: a foreign term for a topical stamp.

tied: indicates that a single cancellation strike falls on both stamp and cover. Such a stamp is said to be "tied to cover."

topical: a stamp related to a topic such as birds, flowers, medicine, sports, etc. Topical collectors form collections of stamps relating to their chosen theme.

transit mark: a marking applied to a cover at a point along its journey.

Universal Postal Union (UPU): international postal governing body to which all recognized nations belong. The UPU administers postal treaties and the transmission of mail between member states. Founded in 1863.

ungummed: without gum. Usually implying the stamp was issued without gum.

unlisted: not recognized by a catalogue publisher as being a postage stamp, either by virtue of having been issued by an entity not recognized as a legitimate government or not having been issued for postal purposes.

unused: not cancelled, but not necessarily possessing original gum or in mint condition. *See* **mint**.

unwatermarked: not possessing a watermark. *See* **watermark**.

used: cancelled.

viewcard: a commercially produced card containing an illustration (often a landmark, landscape, or building, but also a humorous message or greeting) and usually sold or given as a souvenir. Also called a picture postcard.

vignette: pronounced vin-yet. The central portion of a stamp design appearing inside an outer frame or border, usually a portrait or scene.

wallpaper: common, inexpensive, colorful stamps of the type sold in bulk and having little individual value.

want list: a list given to dealers or fellow collectors itemizing stamps one is interested in acquiring.

water-activated gum: stamp gum made sticky by the application of moisture, such as saliva. Stamps possessing water-activated gum are sometimes called lick-and-stick stamps, as opposed to those with self-adhesive gum.

watermark: a design impressed into paper during its manufacture, sometimes visible when held up to light, but most often visible when immersed in watermark fluid.

wet gum: gum that is shiny or glossy in appearance, as opposed to "dry" gum, which is flat in appearance.

wet printing: intaglio printing utilizing paper dampened in order to make it receptive to ink. Paper used for wet printing usually has a moisture content of 15 to 35 percent; paper used for "dry" printing usually contains only 5 to 10 percent moisture content. Wet-printed stamps usually appear flat and lackluster when compared to dry-printed stamps. *See* **dry printing**.

wove paper: a finely textured, smooth paper. The most common type of paper, both within and outside philately.

wrapper: a piece of postal stationery used to wrap periodicals for mailing, and in the philatelic sense, usually with postage pre-printed on it.

ZIP: as in Zip Code, an acronym that originally stood for Zone Improvement Plan when first introduced in 1963.

RESOURCE GUIDE

ALBUMS, MOUNTS & SUPPLIES (Manufacturers)

H. E. Harris & Co.
P.O. Box 817, Florence, AL 35631; (800) 528-3992; fax: (205) 766-7058.
Albums, mounts, supplies.

Krause Publications
700 East State Street, Iola, WI 54990; (715) 445-2214; fax: (715) 445-4087; website: www.collectit.net.
Albums and supplements.

Lighthouse Publications, Inc.
P.O. Box 705, Hackensack, NJ 07602-0705; (201) 342-1513.
Albums, mounts, supplies.

Lindner Publications, Inc.
P.O. Box 5056, Syracuse, NY 13220, (315) 437-0463; fax (315) 437-4832; website: www.lindner-usa.com.
Albums, mounts, supplies.

Safe Publications, Inc.
P.O. Box 263, Southampton, PA 18966; (215) 357-9049; fax: (215) 357-5202; website: www.safepub.com.
Albums, mounts, supplies.

Scott Publishing Company
P.O. Box 828, Sidney, OH 45365; (937) 498-0802; fax (937) 498-0807; website: www.scottonline.com.
Albums, mounts, supplies.

Vidiforms, Inc.
115 North Route 9W, Congers, NY 10920; (914) 268-4005; fax: (914) 268-5324.
Albums, mounts, supplies.

Washington Press
2 Vreeland Road, Florham Park, NJ 07932; website: www.washpress.com.
ArtCraft first day covers; White Ace album pages; Stampmounts.

ALBUMS, MOUNTS & SUPPLIES (Direct Mail)

Freeway Supplies
1111 East Truslow Avenue, Fullerton, CA 92831; (800) 447-8100; (714) 447-8100; fax: (714) 680-0962; website: www.freewaysupplies.com.
Albums, mounts, supplies.

Potomac Supplies
7720 Wisconsin Avenue, Bethesda, MD 20814; (301) 654-8828; fax: (301) 654-1923; website: www.potomacsupplies.com.
Albums, mounts, supplies.

Subway Stamp Shop
2121 Beale Avenue, Altoona, PA 16601; (800) 221-9960, (814) 946-1000; fax (814) 946-9997; website: www.subwaystamp.com.
Albums, mounts, supplies.

DEALER ORGANIZATIONS

American Stamp Dealers Association (ASDA)
3 School Street, Suite 205, Glen Cove, NY 11542-2548; (516) 759-7000; fax (516) 759-7014; website: www.amerstampdlrs.com.
Dealer guide and dealer referral service.

American Philatelic Society (APS)
P.O. Box 8000, State College, PA 16803; (814) 237-3803; website: www.stamps.org.
Dealer guide.

National Stamp Dealers Association (NSDA)
P.O. Box 7176, Redwood City, CA 94063; (800) 875-6633.

DIRECTORIES

Yellow Pages for Stamp Collectors
Linn's Stamp News, P.O. Box 29, Sidney, OH 45365; (937) 498-0801; website: www.linns.com.

Where to Buy It Guide to the Stamp World
Krause Publications, 700 East State Street, Iola, WI 54990; (715) 445-2214; fax: (715) 445-4087; website: www.collectit.net.

EXPERTIZING

American Philatelic Expertizing Service (APEX)
P.O. Box 8000, State College, PA 16803; (814) 237-3803.
Send for submission forms before submitting stamps.

Philatelic Foundation
501 Fifth Avenue, Room 1901, New York, NY 10017; (212) 867-3699.
Send for submission forms before submitting stamps.

MUSEUMS

Hall of Stamps
United States Postal Service, 475 L'Enfant Plaza, Washington, DC 20260.

National Postal Museum
Smithsonian Institution, 2 Massachusetts Avenue NE, Washington, DC 20560.

Spellman Museum of Stamps and Postal History
235 Wellsley Street, Weston, MA 02193; (781) 768-8367; website:
www.spellman.org.

MAGAZINES

American Philatelist
P.O. Box 8000, State College, PA 16803.
Monthly journal of the American Philatelic Society.

Mekeel's and Stamps Magazine (weekly)
P.O. Box 5050, White Plains, NY 10602; (800) 635-3351; fax:
(914) 997-7261.

NEWSPAPERS

Global Stamp News (monthly)
P.O. Box 97, Sidney, OH 45365; (937) 492-3183; fax: (937) 492-
6514.
*Devoted to foreign stamps. Bargain-priced subscription rate, plus
lots of ads for packets and approvals. Great for the beginner,
generalist, or advanced collector.*

Linn's Stamp News (weekly)
P.O. Box 29, Sidney, OH 45365; (937) 498-0801; website:
www.linns.com.
General newspaper covering all aspects of philately.

Scott Stamp Monthly
P.O. Box 828, Sidney, OH 45365; (937) 498-0802; fax: (937) 498-
0807; website: www.scottonline.com.
Excellent publication with articles of interest to all levels.

Stamp Collector (bi-monthly)
700 East State Street, Iola, WI 54990; (715) 445-2214; fax: (715)
445-4087; website: www.collectit.net.
General newspaper covering all aspects of philately.

PHILATELIC AGENCIES

Hundreds of foreign philatelic agencies exist from which new issues can be purchased at face value. Complete listings are published from time to time in philatelic periodicals.

Philatelic Fulfillment Service Center (USPS)
United States Postal Service, Box 419424, Kansas City, MO 64141-6424; (800) 782-6724; website: www.stampsonline.com.

PHILATELIC LIBRARIES

American Philatelic Research Library (APRL)
100 Oakwood Avenue, State College, PA 16803; (814) 237-3803; fax: (814) 237-6128; website: www.stamps.org.
One of the largest collections of philatelic books in the world. Open to the public; borrowing by members only.

Baltimore Philatelic Society Library
1224 North Calvert Street, Baltimore, MD 21202; (410) 226-8598.

Calgary Philatelic Society Library
6219 Dalton Drive, NW, Calgary, Alberta T3A 1E1, Canada.

The Collectors Club Library
22 East 35th Street, New York, NY 10016-3806; (212) 683-0559; fax: (212) 481-1269.
Open to the public; borrowing by members only.

The Postal History Foundation
920 North First Avenue, P.O. Box 40724, Tucson, AZ 85717; (520) 623-6652.

Rocky Mountain Philatelic Library
2038 South Pontiac Way, Denver, CO 80224; (303) 759-9921.

San Diego County Philatelic Library
4133 Poplar Street, San Diego, CA 92105.

Smithsonian Institution Libraries
National Postal Museum Branch, Smithsonian Institution, Washington, DC 20560; (408) 733-0336.

Spellman Museum Philatelic Library
235 Wellsley Street, Weston, MA 02193; (781) 768-8367; website: www.spellman.org.

Western Philatelic Library
Room 6, Building 6, 1500 Partridge Avenue, Sunnyvale, CA 94087; (408) 733-0336.

Vincent Graves Greene Philatelic Research Library
First Canadian Place, Box 100, Toronto, Ontario M5X 1S2, Canada.

Wineburgh Philatelic Research Library
University of Texas at Dallas
P.O. Box 830643, Richardson, TX 75083-0643; (214) 883-2570; fax: (214) 883-2473.

PHILATELIC LITERATURE DEALERS
Philip T. Bansner, Inc.
P.O. Box 2529, West Lawn, PA 19609; (610) 678-5000; fax: (610) 678-5400; website: www.philbansner.com.
Inventory of 5,000 new and out-of-print titles.

PHILATELIC SOCIETIES
Check with the American Philatelic Society for addresses of affiliate societies, or check in the front of the latest Scott Specialized Catalogue of U.S. Stamps *for current society addresses.*

American Philatelic Society (APS)
P.O. Box 8000, State College, PA 16803; (814) 237-3803; website: www.stamps.org.

Errors, Freaks, Oddities Collectors Club (EFOCC)
138 Lakemont Drive East, Kingsland, GA 31548-8921;
fax: (912) 729-1585.

STAMP DEALERS (Approval)

Numerous approval dealers do business in the United States. The following includes several of the oldest and largest. Philatelic periodicals contain names of numerous others.

Jamestown Stamp Company
341 East Third Street, Jamestown, NY 14701; (716) 488-0763; fax: (716) 664-2211; website: www.jamestownstamp.com.

Kenmore Stamp Company
119 West Street, Milford, NH 03055; (800) 225-5059; (603) 673-1745; fax: (603) 673-3222.

Mystic Stamp Company
9700 Mill Street, Camden, NY 13316; (315) 245-2690; fax: (315) 245-0036.

STAMP DEALERS (Local)

Far too numerous to list. Consult your telephone Yellow Pages.

STAMP INSURANCE

American Philatelic Society
Insurance Advisor
P.O. Box 8000, State College, PA 16803; (814) 237-3803; fax: (814) 237-6128.

Collectibles Insurance Agency
P.O. Box 1200, Westminster, MD 21158; (888) 837-9537; fax: (410) 876-9233; website: www.collectinsure.com.

BIBLIOGRAPHY

CATALOGUES

Brookman Disney Price Guide. Brookman Stamp Company, 10 Chestnut Drive, Bedford, NH 03110. *Complete catalogue/pricelist of stamps featuring Disney characters and subjects.*

Brookman United States, United Nations & Canada Stamps & Postal Collectibles. Brookman Stamp Company, 10 Chestnut Drive, Bedford, NH 03110. *Stamp price guide. Published annually.*

Catalogue of Errors on U. S. Postage Stamps. Krause Publications, 700 East State Street, Iola, WI 54990. *Comprehensive catalogue of U.S. major error stamps, fully illustrated, includes section on EFOs. Published annually.*

Comprehensive Catalogue of United States Stamp Booklets. Robert Furman. Krause Publications, 700 East State Street, Iola, WI 54990. *Comprehensive listings and values for all U.S. booklets and booklet panes from the first issue onward, including varieties. Profusely illustrated.*

Durland Standard Plate Number Catalog. Bureau Issues Association, P.O. Box 23707, Belleville, IL 62223. *The most comprehensive listing of U.S. plate blocks. Lists every known plate block by number and position. Illustrated.*

Harris US/BNA Postage Stamp Catalog. H.E. Harris & Co., P.O. Box 817, Florence, AL 35631. *Catalogue/pricelist for U.S. and British North America. Published annually.*

Krause-Minkus Standard Catalog of U.S. Stamps. Krause Publications, 700 East State Street, Iola, WI 54990. *Catalogue of U.S. stamps featuring a wealth of information about each issue. Published annually.*

Mystic U.S. Stamp Catalogue. Mystic Stamp Company, 24 Mill Street, Camden, NY 13116-9111. *Catalogue of U.S. stamps featuring full-color illustrations.*

Planty Photo Encyclopedia of Cacheted First Day Covers. Earl Planty. Michael A. Mellone, P.O. Box 206, Stewartsville, NJ 08886. *Highly detailed multi-volume catalogue on cacheted FDCs of the classic period, 1901-1939.*

The Postal Service Guide to U.S. Stamps. United States Postal Service, Box 419636, Kansas City, MO 64179-0996. *Noteworthy for its full-color illustrations. Available by mail, but also available at many post offices and most philatelic windows.*

Sanabria Airmail Catalogue. Krause Publications, 700 East State Street, Iola, WI 54990. *Catalogue of airmail stamps of the world.*

Scott Standard Postage Stamp Catalogue. Scott Publishing Co., P.O. Box 828, Sidney, OH 45365. *Multi-volume set listing all postage stamps of the world. Published annually.*

Scott U.S. First Day Cover Catalogue and Checklist. Mike Mellone. Scott Publishing Co., P.O. Box 828, Sidney, OH 45365. *Detailed listings for U.S. first day covers. Published annually.*

Scott Specialized Catalogue of U.S. Stamps and Covers. Scott Publishing Co., P.O. Box 828, Sidney, OH 45365. *Detailed, comprehensive listing of all U.S. postage stamps, postal stationery, revenue stamps, and more. Published annually.*

Town & Type Catalogue. Precancel Stamp Society, PSS Catalogs, 108 Ashswamp Road, Scarborough, ME 04074. *Complete listing of all recognized U.S. precancels.*

ELECTRONIC MEDIA

AlbumPro. The Well-Centered Publishing Company, P.O. Box 8459, Greenville, SC 29604; website: www.albumpro.com. *Album page design software with clip art and graphics import capability. Highly rated.*

Linn's Guide to Stamp Collecting Software. William F. Sharpe. Linn's Stamp News, P.O. Box 29, Sidney, OH 45365; website: www.linns.com. *Rates and evaluates software, includes chapters on hardware, CD-ROMs, stamp inventory programs, album page creation, plus stamp collecting sites on the Internet. Loaded with practical information.*

Scott U.S. Stamp Collector's Database. Scott Publishing Company, P.O. Box 828, Sidney, OH 45365; website: www.scottonline.com. *Basically a stamp catalogue CD-ROM with prices and full-color images of U.S. stamps, plus inventory feature and want-list feature.*

Stamp Collector's Data Base. SCDB Software, Inc., 8505 River Rock Terrace, Suite B, Bethesda, MD 20817. *Database software inventory system for Windows or DOS, featuring annual catalogue value updates, includes full-color stamp images and want-list features, accommodates yearly updates.*

StampBase with StampPics. Changing Seasons Software, Ltd., 5881 Roanoke Drive, Madison, WI 53719; website: www.stampbase.com. *Database software, stamp inventory system for Windows featuring annual catalogue value updates, includes full-color stamp images and want-list features.*

StampTRAC. StampFinder, 6175 N.W. 153rd Street, Suite 201, Miami Lakes, FL 33014; website: www.stampfinder.com. *Free downloadable database inventory software.*

GENERAL READING

Basic Philately. Kenneth A. Wood. Krause Publications, 700 East State Street, Iola, WI 54990.

Facts and Fantasy About Philately. John M. Hotchner. P.O. Box 1125, Falls Church, VA 22041. *Delightful book of stamp-collecting wit and wisdom by one of America's best-known philatelic columnists and writers. Especially recommended for beginners.*

Fun and Profit in Stamp Collecting. Herman Herst, Jr. Linn's Stamp News, P.O. Box 29, Sidney, OH 45365. *Informative and thoroughly enjoyable look into the world of stamps and money by one of America's best-loved philatelic writers.*

Franklin D. Roosevelt & the Stamps of the United States 1933-1945. Brian C. Baur. Linn's Stamp News, P.O. Box 29, Sidney, OH 45365. *Rare, behind-the-scenes look at the origins of some of America's best-loved stamps and the stamp-collecting President's input into their creation.*

Fundamentals of Philately. L.N. Williams. American Philatelic Society, P.O. Box 8000, State College, PA 16803. *An 880-page masterwork loaded with information of use to every philatelist from beginner to specialist. Hundreds of illustrations.*

Linn's U.S. Stamp Yearbook. Linn's Stamp News, P.O. Box 29, Sidney, OH 45355. *Published annually since 1983, loaded with massive detail about design, alternate designs, varieties, stamp production, problems, and more, for each stamp issued each year.*

Nassau Street. Herman Herst, Jr. Linn's Stamp News, P.O. Box 29, Sidney, OH 45365. *Enjoyable memoir of a stamp dealer active during the golden era of philately. Philately's all-time best-selling book is a must-read for anyone—beginner and advanced collector alike—who collects stamps.*

On The Road: The Quest for Stamps. Stephen R. Datz. General Philatelic Corporation, P.O. Box 402, Loveland, CO 80539. *A stamp dealer's entertaining true-life adventures while on the road buying stamp collections from the public all across America.*

Philatelic Forgers: Their Lives and Works. Varro E. Tyler. Linn's Stamp News, P.O. Box 29, Sidney, OH 45365. *Intriguing narrative of some of the most famous and prolific philatelic forgers. The most comprehensive work on the men who faked stamps and the stamps they faked.*

Spurious Stamps: A History of U.S. Postal Counterfeits. H.K. Petschel. American Philatelic Society, P.O. Box 8000, State College, PA 16803. *Fascinating history of postal fraud from 1895 into the 1970s written by a retired postal inspector. Includes color plates of fakes.*

Still More Stories to Collect Stamps By. Herman Herst, Jr. Mekeel's Stamp News, P.O. Box 5050, White Plains, NY 10602. *More stories by the best-selling author of* Nassau Street.

The Wild Side: Philatelic Mischief, Murder, and Intrigue. Stephen R. Datz. General Philatelic Corporation, P.O. Box 402, Loveland, CO 80539. *Veteran stamp dealer's real-life experiences with a rogues' gallery of scoundrels, eccentrics, and misfits from the side of philately the public seldom sees.*

The World's Greatest Stamp Collectors. Stanley M. Bierman. Linn's Stamp News, P.O. Box 29, Sidney, OH 45365. *Highly readable biographies of the world's greatest stamps collectors.*

More of the World's Greatest Stamp Collectors. Stanley M. Bierman. Linn's Stamp News, P.O. Box 29, Sidney, OH 45365. *Companion volume to the above.*

REFERENCE GUIDES

Affordable Foreign Errors.   Paul S. Greenlaw, with Martin Sellinger.   Krause Publications, 700 East State Street, Iola, WI 54990. *Comprehensive guide to identifying and collecting foreign stamp errors, many of which are readily affordable.*

American Stamp Dealers Association Membership Guide. American Stamp Dealers Association, 3 School Street, Glen Cove, NY 11452-2548.   *Guide to stamp dealers in America cross referenced by specialty.*

The Buyer's Guide to Selected U.S. Postage Stamps. Stephen R. Datz. General Philatelic Corporation, P.O. Box 402, Loveland, CO 80539. *Highly detailed, stamp-by-stamp analysis of quality U.S. stamps for the selective buyer, including premium characteristics, gum and hinging, fakes and problem stamps, when to expertize, etc. Completely illustrated.*

How to Detect Damaged, Altered, and Repaired Stamps. Paul W. Schmid.   Krause Publications, 700 East State Street, Iola, WI 54990. *The most authoritative and easy-to-use book on the subject of altered U.S. stamps. Well illustrated. Highly recommended.*

International Encyclopedic Dictionary of Philately.   R. Scott Carlton.   Krause Publications, 700 East State Street, Iola, WI 54990. *Offers more than 1,000 sources for further research on stamp collecting terms including English translation of foreign terms.*

Linn's Plate Number Coil Handbook. Ken Lawrence. Linn's Stamp News, P.O. Box 29, Sidney, OH 45365. *The definitive work on this popular specialty. Copiously illustrated.*

Mekeel's U.S. Reference Manual. Mekeel's Stamp News, P.O. Box 5050, White Plains, NY 10602. *In-depth look at selected U.S. special-interest stamps and covers, including rarities and difficult-to-identify items.*

Micarelli Identification Guide to U.S. Stamps. Charles Micarelli. Scott Publishing Co., P.O. Box 828, Sidney, OH 45365. *Comprehensive identification guide to U.S. definitive stamps, fully illustrated, and especially useful for hard-to-identify nineteenth-century issues.*

Post Dates. Kenneth A. Wood. Krause Publications, 700 East State Street, Iola, WI 54990. *A 400-page chronology of more than 6,000 intriguing events in the mails and philately beginning with the year 4,000 BC.*

Stamp Investing. Stephen R. Datz. General Philatelic Corporation, P.O. Box 402, Loveland, CO 80539. *Comprehensively covers all aspects of stamps as investments.*

StampFinders Stamp Selection Guides. USID, Inc., 6175 N.W. 153rd Street, Suite 201, Miami Lakes, FL 33014. *Investment oriented stamp price performance guides. Volumes include U.S. and Canada; British Commonwealth; Mexico and South America; Germany and German Colonies; and the Far East.*

This is Philately; An Encyclopedia of Stamp Collecting. Kenneth A. Wood. Krause Publications, 700 East State Street, Iola, WI 54990. *Superb three-volume reference covering every conceivable aspect of philately.*

Top Dollar Paid: The Complete Guide to Selling Your Stamps. Stephen R. Datz. General Philatelic Corporation, P.O. Box 402, Loveland, CO 80539. *Best-selling how-to guide loaded with practical information and entertaining narrative about the stamp business. Not only for sellers, but for all who buy or collect stamps.*

Triangular Philatelics. Charles Green. Krause Publications, 700 East State Street, Iola, WI 54990. *Guide for collectors interested in this perennially popular topic, includes listings for every country that ever issued triangular stamps.*

United States Postal History Sampler. Richard B. Graham. Linn's Stamp News, P.O. Box 29, Sidney, OH 45365. *Fascinating introduction to the world of U.S. postal history. Profusely illustrated.*

U.S. Stamp Facts, 19th Century. Linn's Stamp News, P.O. Box 29, Sidney, OH 45365. *Detailed listings for important stamps of the nineteenth century. Devotes a page to each stamp and includes information on plate numbers, plate arrangement, quantity issued, earliest known use, number of surviving covers, and more. Fully illustrated. Recommended for any buyer of nineteenth-century U.S. stamps.*

Where in the World? Krause Publications, 700 East State Street, Iola, WI 54990. *Comprehensive and useful atlas of stamp-issuing entities since 1840.*

INDEX

MORE GOOD READING
BY STEPHEN R. DATZ

TOP DOLLAR PAID!
The best selling book about buying and selling stamps. It's two books in one: a concise factual guide, and an entertaining, revealing behind-the-scenes narrative about the real-life world of stamp dealing written by a dealer with decades of experience. Critically acclaimed, it's an absolute must-read for anyone who buys, collects, or invests, as well as anyone thinking about selling a stamp collection.
ISBN 0-88219-022-9 $14.95

THE WILD SIDE
The second in Datz's trilogy about the stamp business. An eye-opening journey into the side of stamp dealing you never hear about. Datz's first-hand (and often not-so-pleasant) encounters with philatelic con-men, crooks, and scammers. Meet a rogues' gallery of shadowy characters, eccentrics, and even murderers—all real people inhabiting the dark underside of philately. You won't be able to put it down.
ISBN 0-88219-024-5 $9.95

ON THE ROAD
The third in Datz's trilogy. Datz's true-life adventures chasing stamp deals all over the map from the desolate hinterlands of Wyoming and Montana to the bright lights of Las Vegas and New York. An amazing odyssey: fast times and big-dollar deals, wild goose chases and third-rate motels, blizzards and tornados, eccentric millionaires and desert rats, even hippie hitchhikers. Action packed all the way. You'll be up all night finishing this one.
ISBN 0-88129-025-3 $9.95

THE BUYERS GUIDE
A **must** for every buyer of premium quality U.S. stamps. Covers every important U.S. stamp (more than 600) and includes: a stamp-by-stamp analysis of premium characteristics; gum and hinging; centering and margins; color and freshness; faults and imperfections; warnings about fakes and problem stamps; when to expertize; quantities NH vs. hinged; frequency at auction; completely illustrated. A powerhouse of knowledge—the kind professionals carry inside their heads—at your fingertips in a convenient, easy-to-use handbook.
ISBN 0-88219-026-1 $14.95

STAMP INVESTING
The essential guide to profit in stamp investing. Includes: economics of the stamp market; basic strategies and tactics; speculative strategies; spotting profit opportunities; utilizing statistical tools; how and when to buy right—and sell right; stamp investment myths; Wall Street and stamps; scams and rip-offs to avoid; plus much more. If you enjoy stamps, there's no reason why you shouldn't profit from them, too.
ISBN 0-88219-029-6 $14.95

Available from your local bookseller
or directly from the publisher.

GENERAL PHILATELIC CORPORATION
P. O. Box 402
Loveland, CO 80539

(Postage & handling $2 for the first book, $1 for each additional book.)